Covenants and Pinky Promises

Covenants and Pinky Promises

PUTTING THE I INTO INTEGRITY

Dr. Eva S. Benevento

Covenants and Pinky Promises:
Putting the I into Integrity

All Scripture quotation, unless otherwise indicated, are taken from the New American Standard Bible (NASB)®. © Copyright 1960, 1962, 1963, 1968, 1971, 1972, 1973, 1975, 1977. Used by permission. (www.Lockman.org.).

Scriptures marked KJV are taken from the King James Version (KJV): King James Version, public domain.

© 2017 Dr. Eva S. Benevento

All rights reserved. No part of this book may be reproduced or used in any form or by any means, electronic or mechanical, without written permission from the publisher. The author has made every effort to provide accurate information, Internet addresses, and any other contact information at the time of publication. Neither the publisher nor the author assumes responsibility for errors or changes that occur after publication. The publisher or author does not have control over or responsibility for third-party websites or their content.

ISBN: 0692980202
ISBN 13: 9780692980200
Library of Congress Control Number: 2017917530
Eva Benevento, Ramsey, NJ

Endorsements

THIS IS AN EXCELLENT BOOK to read: Spirit-filled, insightful, and truth-telling in God's love. This extraordinary work zeroes in on the core value of all relationships: receiving purity and integrity from Above and keeping our sacred covenants and promises in our broken world. I love this book, full of biblical insights, transformative stories, and spiritual wisdom. Dr. Eva Benevento, a person of integrity, guides us on how we can authentically keep our covenants and live a life of integrity by the power of Holy Spirit. This precious book provides an indispensable resource for youth, young adults, and married couples. I would wholeheartedly recommend this book to all Christians who desire to be trustworthy covenant builders.

Dr. Andrew Sung Park,
Professor of Theology at United Theological Seminary, Dayton, Ohio;
author, *The Wounded Heart of God: The Asian Concept of Han and the Christian Doctrine of Sin* and *Triune Atonement: Christ's Healing for Sinners, Victims, and the Whole Creation.*

We live in an age of broken promises where a person's word is seldom any longer his or her bond. Dr. Benevento has given wise counsel on a living a life of integrity, blending in-depth study of biblical truth regarding covenants and promises with insightful practical application and relevant, real-life illustrations for sticky life situations. I have known Eva for several years, first as my student in a doctoral program, then as a colleague in ministry, and I can affirm that she is a woman of integrity, living out what she writes about. You will grow in mind and spirit through this book and will be challenged to be a person of integrity.

Paul L. King, Th.D., D.Min.,
pastor, author, professor,
Faculty Director of Ratio Christi/Purdue Christian Faculty
& Staff Network.

Eva Benevento's new work on the implications of the biblical covenants reminds me of my wedding vows I wrote that emphasized the obligation of mirroring a covenant-*making*, and covenant-*keeping* God in our relationship. (The marriage worked out quite well). Christians are called to be covenant-keepers. This book explores the various directions this principle must take if we are to reflect the character of our Father in Heaven. In a day when fidelity to our national covenant, the Constitution, is ridiculed as the deceitful product of dead, white, Christian, racist slave-holders, we now, more than ever, need to return to the biblical cohesive force that makes a republic--and indeed, civilization--possible: that is, the will to make and keep honest promises.

Dr. Jon Ruthven,
Professor Emeritus, Theology from Regent
University School of Divinity;
author, *What's Wrong with Protestant Theology* and
On the Cessation of the Charismata.

Covenants and Pinky Promises: Putting the I into Integrity reveals the way to living a life and lifestyle of integrity. Dr. Benevento's book reveals and releases the anointing for each of these four concepts in the title to be desired, pursued, and formed in one's character. The following quotation is very significant: ". . . the Old and New Covenants reveal the integrity of God's word to His people, and His character to faithfully execute that which He has covenanted."

Dr. Bobbie Jean Merck,
founder of A Great Love Inc., Toccoa, Georgia;
author, *Power of the Secret Place; Ask of Me,* and more.

In a time that denies cause and effect, Dr. Benevento offers this profound, readable, and specific call to live with integrity in every area of life, so that we can know God and love each other well. It comes back to covenants, promises that we make, but the secret that sets us free is that God keeps His promises to us, even when we go back on our word. Read this gem and expect a fresh start for yourself!

Dr. Gerard Labrecque,
Staunton, Virginia,
presenter of Holy Spirit-Fired Dream Interpretation at the
45th Annual Meeting of the Society for Pentecostal Studies, 2016.

God is a God of covenants. The Bible is a book of covenants. But covenants are no better than the integrity of the people who make them. I've known Eva and her husband Ben for several years. I know of no other couple that model integrity better than they do. That is why I'm excited about her latest book. For Eva, this is not just a theory but an outgrowth of how she lives her life. My prayer is that as you read this book that you will become a person of integrity that models the faithfulness of our Father.

Dr. Geoffrey Wattoff,
Centereach, New York

Dr. Benevento's newest book is a worthy addition to any library, Christian and non-Christian. It is a much needed reminder and recall to a time when honor and integrity were not seen as strictly Christian concepts. It was a time when the course of civilizations was set into motion with a simple handshake, and a "gentleman's agreement" was worth more than the voluminous contracts of today—contracts with built-in expectation of deceit and failure. The character and structure of Dr. Benevento's writing is reminiscent of Norman Vincent Peale and C.S. Lewis, as it crosses religious, cultural and social lines, gently reminding us that we all share a common history of "pinky promises." It is, as such, a beacon of light in an increasingly polarized world.

Dr. Wendy Chojnowski-Olson,
Evanston, Illinois

Covenants and Pinky Promises: Putting the I into Integrity is a must read for every disciple of Jesus Christ! Dr. Eva Benevento is an incredibly gifted writer and has diligently researched on the subject of integrity. I love how this book is written from both a biblical and intellectual standpoint. This book gives the reader life's lessons where promise keeping and agreements are made, kept, and when broken, gives encouragement that restoration is always possible.

Rev. Margie Fleurant,
President and Founder of The River Ministries

Dedication

*To Anthony, known as "Ben" to family and friends,
lover of God,
wonderful husband and amazing father to our children,
because you live the meaning of covenant.*

Acknowledgements

WRITING THIS BOOK IS A product of grace and inspiration as a believer and follower of Jesus, and my relationship with the Holy Spirit. As I gathered my thoughts, I found myself being led to specific stories and passages in God's Word that exemplify the point. Simple memories of my own life emerged and are sprinkled throughout the chapters.

Family and friends have added to God's grace for this project in time, prayer, and encouragement. Besides my husband and kids, there are some people who have touched this project with brilliant feedback, suggestions, and endorsements—you know who you are, and so does our heavenly Father, who I pray will reward you bountifully. I don't think I can say this enough, but a deeply felt "thank you" stated here is in metaphoric neon lights and fireworks. Thank you for your friendship and generosity, and for making heaven happy because of it.

Table of Contents

Endorsements · v
Dedication ·ix
Acknowledgements· ·xi
Abbreviations · xv
Introduction · xvii

A Promise is a Promise· 1
Unravel the "Legalese" · 9
The Power of Covenant Words · 29
Relational Covenants · 47
Intimate Covenants · 62
Marketplace Covenants · 81
Remembering Covenants· 93
Putting the "I" Into Integrity · 101

About the Author · 111

Abbreviations
BOOKS OF THE BIBLE IN ALPHABETICAL ORDER

OLD TESTAMENT		NEW TESTAMENT	
Amos	Am	Acts of the Apostles	Acts
1 Chronicles	1 Chr	Colossians	Col
2 Chronicles	2 Chr	1 Corinthians	1 Cor
Daniel	Dn	2 Corinthians	2 Cor
Deuteronomy	Dt	Ephesians	Eph
Ecclesiastes	Eccl	Galatians	Gal
Esther	Est	Hebrews	Heb
Exodus	Ex	James	Jas
Ezekiel	Ez	John	Jn
Ezra	Ezr	1 John	1 Jn
Genesis	Gn	2 John	2 Jn
Habakkuk	Hb	3 John	3 Jn
Haggai	Hg	Jude	Jude
Hosea	Hos	Luke	Lk
Isaiah	Is	Mark	Mk
Jeremiah	Jer	Matthew	Mt
Job	Jb	1 Peter	1 Pt
Joel	Jl	2 Peter	2 Pt
Jonah	Jon	Philippians	Phil
Joshua	Jo	Philemon	Phlm
Judges	Jgs	Revelation	Rev
1 Kings	1 Kgs	Romans	Rom
2 Kings	2 Kgs	1 Thessalonians	1 Thes
Lamentations	Lam	2 Thessalonians	2 Thes
Leviticus	Lv	1 Timothy	1 Tim
Malachi	Mal	2 Timothy	2 Tim
Micah	Mi	Titus	Ti
Nahum	Na		
Nehemiah	Neh		
Numbers	Nm		
Obadiah	Ob		
Proverbs	Prv		
Psalms	Ps (Plural Pss)		
Ruth	Ru		
1 Samuel	1 Sm		
2 Samuel	2 Sm		
Song of Solomon	Sg		
Zechariah	Zec		
Zephaniah	Zep		

Introduction

Who has not been disappointed in some measure as a result of broken promises, untrustworthy relationships, or betrayals. Lack of integrity does not discriminate—it can be found in small or large degrees among family, friends, business associates, government, and even church people. My share in the foibles of humanity has prompted this writing and is intended to challenge all of us to holy living, particularly in the area of promise keeping.

Integrity can sound like a lofty ideal—an intangible fuzzy something that you know when you see it, but can't quite fully explain. To better understand what that looks like, we need to know what it is and what it's not. A simple definition according to www.dictionary.com is "adherence to moral and ethical principles; soundness of moral character; honesty." Some synonyms for integrity that fill out its meaning include candor, forthrightness, goodness, honor, incorruptibility, purity, rectitude, uprightness. The opposite of each of these tell what integrity is not, which include deceit, corruption, disgrace, dishonor, and incompleteness. The examples of these components in our everyday interactions give applicable and tangible witness of the meaning of integrity because it's easier to point out when someone acts with integrity or when they don't. We've all experienced both and recognize it when we see it.

The organization of this book is fairly simple. Sorting out the language of agreement begins the investigation. Life's lessons where promise-keeping and agreements are made, kept, and sometimes broken are found in many contexts—personal, business, and spiritual. Each chapter discusses a central focus of covenant-keeping between God and humanity, as well as for people between one another. As a practical approach to bringing about restoration and encouragement, each chapter ends with a section entitled "The Good News," and "Prayer," which prompts practical life application of the chapter's content. At the end of the book, a guide containing questions for each chapter can be used for group discussion or personal journaling.

Nobody can claim having arrived at perfection in this life, but we are on a journey that includes ongoing self-assessment and Holy Spirit conviction in areas that need change—repentance, commitment, and restoration, be it in simple or complex matters. These few chapters invite you to take another look at where you have been, where you are, and where you are going in strengthening relationships by practicing the art of promise-keeping and living a life that reflects the integrity you were meant to live. It's a journey worth taking and promises great rewards.

A Promise is a Promise

Pinky Promises

CHILDREN ARE AMAZING. THEY OFTEN understand the uncomplicated truth easier than adults. As children, my friends and I made promises now and then. We would lock pinky fingers with each other and called them "pinky promises." A pinky promise was serious business. It was a promise you simply did not break because you trusted your friend without measure. Broken pinky promises meant you risked severed friendships.

Child trust is uncomplicated. Their innocence makes them both endearing and vulnerable. In Mt 19:14, Jesus invites children to come to Him and says, ". . . for such is the kingdom of heaven." He calls us to come to Him with the simplicity of a child who so easily believes. We become children of God by simple uncomplicated faith in Christ (Gal 3:26), and receive all that He has for us by faith because He is faithful to His promises—way better than pinky promises.

What is the value of a promise? We've all experienced how frustrating it is when people make promises, having good intentions for the moment, but then do not follow through. Trust is eroded. It can be about simple things like chronically showing up late, dates for lunch or dinner repeatedly broken, or the promised phone call that never comes. Broken promises treated as no big deal add insult to injury.

What good is someone's word if it is not backed by action? We hold companies accountable for their shortcomings on pledges, but do we hold ourselves accountable with the same expectations for both the big things or even the little ones? Trust is the confident expectation of something promised, the reliance on certainty. Trust is a precious commodity and loyalty is built on a history of a reliable "yes" being "yes," and "no" being "no."

Besides building good relationships between individuals, trust is the glue that secures contracts, covenants, and testaments in a broader sense within society and generations. In a society that has become exponentially litigious, the need for contracts have broadened the legal profession to epic proportions. Not everyone who graduates from law school secures a job at a high power legal firm, but there seems to be enough work for an army of attorneys. The number of lawyers in the U.S. has grown from about 200,000 in the year I was born, to over a whopping 1.3 million—yes, million now, and is still increasing (American Bar Association statistics).

Several factors may enter into these increased numbers. Without doubt the increase in contractual law with the expansion of business both domestic and international accounts for some of the increase in the number of attorneys. Furthermore, the incidence of civil litigation proceedings, including personal injury, breach of contract, and divorce litigation (40% to 50% of all marriages in the U.S. end in divorce) are responsible for a good chunk of the increase as well.

More than ever in a complex world, we rely on legal documents for security in business as well as in personal affairs. We enter into a variety of legally binding agreements—deeds, wills, marriage, and commerce deals—and we look to these contracts as critical protection for fulfilled commitments. When contracts are broken, we assume recompense or satisfaction is due. It gives us a sense of security, certainly in dealings with strangers, but no less important when dealing with friends and relatives.

In recent years, pharmaceutical companies advertise drugs on television, but at the same time, legal firms are alerting the public about mass tort litigation for the damage caused by those same drugs.[1] It looks like

---

[1] Although no specific stats are given as to the increase or status quo of the amount of mass tort litigation, it's hard to imagine that the amount has not increased over the past few years. What is certain is that exposure to the public through the use of television media has increased. Typically, the use of media advertising would increase business, otherwise, why would a business invest in such an expensive means of advertising?

a new form of ambulance chasing. Legal firms are offering to negotiate down tax debt with the IRS, which can be exceptionally irksome to people who pay their full tax debt regularly and on time. These types of debt reduction commercials were unheard of not too many years ago. Our courts are clogged with frivolous suits at the expense of the tax paying public, and furthermore, legitimate court proceedings are often unnecessarily delayed due to the clogged court system. By all means, legitimate cases of loss should require recompense even at the cost of litigation, and attorneys in these cases serve an important role in protecting the rights of both the innocent and guilty, but delay adds to the frustration of litigants.

As a society, we no longer expect people to uphold agreements with a handshake or the words, "I promise." Kindness, understanding, and a desire to get along in peace seem to have vanished in the public arena, neighborhoods, and even among families. Having said that, when it comes to honest dealings, society's loss of integrity is regrettable. Although I lament this state of affairs, we have little choice in this environment but to protect our families and homes, especially from those who use the system to legally extort money when more equitable and less costly solutions could have been reached out of court.

How did we get here? Has there ever been a time when contracts were not necessary? Who is the model for integrity of promises fulfilled? Is there such a thing as an unbreakable contract or covenant? What does God have to say about making and keeping promises and covenants? What is the impact of covenant breaking, and can trust be restored once it has been betrayed? Can we hope to recover principles of honor among humans where their words serve as their bond? Would greater understanding and insight into the God's view of promise-keeping help Bible believers consistently honor their words? What covenants of God are still in effect? These difficult questions prompted this search for insights about promise-making from the perspective of God's Word, and what it means to make and keep promises for human interaction.

In a world where trust is so tenuous, it is a real challenge to visualize integrity as the norm. For a moment, envision a world where all parents, spouses, business associates, church folk, and even politicians, keep their promises and live a life of integrity. If nothing else, it would uncomplicate life significantly. Even so, as followers of Christ, we are called to a discipline of truthful living with integrity and are accountable for how we conduct our lives.

The Good News

If you have been hurt by broken promises, the good news is that you can be free from pain. Memories can remain, but they don't have to hurt. Jesus is the healer of your body and your mind.

"But you don't know what he/she/they did to me!"

"I'll forgive, but I sure won't forget!"

Who hasn't heard these or similar words spoken by someone hurting from an episode of broken promises or even a long-term toxic relationship? Rationalizing the holding on to unforgiveness has profound implications. Some may believe the person who caused them pain deserves vengeance or retribution and that it will somehow ease their pain—the "get even" attitude. In reality, holding onto unforgiveness hurts the victim all over again. It can even impede spiritual growth and the ability to hear the Holy Spirit. When offense begins to take root, like mentally replaying the hurt of broken promises again and again, it becomes a stronghold of bitterness.

Forgiveness does not mean you have to continue a toxic relationship. Forgiveness frees the victim, not necessarily the wrongdoer. If the person who hurt you is not accessible, you can still forgive. If contact is inadvisable as in abusive or criminal situations, you can still forgive. Forgiveness does not absolve a person from the consequences of a criminal act. Justice still demands a penalty for crimes committed. It really is a heart issue, not geography, sociology, or psychology.

The first step is to forgive, and to forgive as quickly as you can. The longer you wait to forgive, the harder it is to forgive. Mark 11:25 states, "Whenever you stand praying, forgive, if you have anything against anyone, so that your Father who is in heaven will also forgive you your transgressions." Forgiving, then, is really a faith act.

The greatest model of forgiveness is Jesus. As He was dying, Jesus said, "Father, forgive them, for they do not know what they are doing" (Lk 23:34a). Forgive and move on. The forgiveness frees us from internal victimization. It frees us from vengeance. Forgiveness positions us to receive a deeper relationship with God, His grace, His provision, and His love.

PRAYER: IF YOU EXPERIENCED BROKEN PROMISES

Lord, you are the great Promise-Keeper, the ever-faithful God who keeps promises. Lord, I receive your comfort and healing of emotional wounds from broken promises. I forgive persons who have hurt me because of their broken promises to me and bless them that they may receive your forgiveness and love. If there is hidden offense or a stronghold in my heart, I ask you, Lord, to forgive me for storing them. I receive your love, forgiveness, and freedom in Jesus' Name.

MORE GOOD NEWS

On the other hand, if you have difficulty keeping your word, the good news is that you can change. That is the meaning of repentance—*metanoeo* in Greek—to change your direction; to change your mind for the better. The power of the Holy Spirit is available to you to strengthen you and guide your life.

First, admit the shortcoming. You cannot change what you are not willing to confront. Instead of feeling condemned, feel convicted and purpose in your heart to renew your mind according to the Word of God. Then receive forgiveness from God on the matter. "If we confess our sins, He is faithful and righteous to forgive us our sins and to cleanse us from all unrighteousness" (1 Jn 1:9). It is the path to walking in freedom.

Where it is possible, make the effort to seek forgiveness and restore broken relationships with humility and right heart, but understand that your effort may not be received by others. Particularly in abusive situations, you may not or perhaps should not have access to those who you hurt. Accept that as consequence of your actions. That should not deter you from seeking forgiveness from God. You cannot control other people's intentions, attitudes, or rights, but you can take charge of yourself and take the necessary steps to rebuild your own life. With God's help, you can become a person of integrity, trust, and truthfulness.

Prayer When You Have Broken Promises to Others
Lord, I ask forgiveness for times when I have not kept my word, and especially when I have caused harm to someone. I ask You, Lord, to bless them with Your love and healing. I believe Your Word brings life to me and my desire is to please you by faith in Your Word. I repent and ask for your strength and guidance to remind me to be a promise-keeper. I welcome You, Holy Spirit, to bring conviction of any unrighteousness in my heart and life. I welcome Your strength, comfort, and guidance to help me repent and be restored. I ask you, Lord, to help me become accountable to my word. Thank you, Lord, that through You, I walk in victory in Jesus' Name.

GUIDE: QUESTIONS FOR DISCUSSION OR JOURNALING

—⚏—

Chapter One: A Promise is a Promise

1. Have you experienced broken promises that left you somewhat jaded and hesitant to trust people? How did you handle it?
2. Have you given your word on something, but then fail to do what you have said? Did it impact you and/or your relationships?
3. How can we confront people in a loving manner who do not keep their promises?
4. Are some promises not worth keeping? Is a broken promise ever a good thing?

Dr. Eva S. Benevento

NOTES

Unravel the "Legalese"

―⚏―

For even the most astute reader, the fine print on legal contracts can be daunting. "Legalese" hails from the complicated world of barristers where every word is scrutinized and justified. Legal words like covenant, promise, testament, agreement, and contract are often used interchangeably by those who are not law-savvy as if they mean the same thing. Each of these words carries a hint of consensus or relationship between parties, but the difference matters. Understanding the differences is helpful to comprehend the context in which they are used.

In most cases the meanings of these words crisscross between biblical and secular contexts. They are worth sorting out. Each word brings new meaning and understanding of the importance of these kinds of interactions.

The words *covenant*, *promise*, and *testament* are frequently used in biblical and secular settings. All three of them carry the meaning of commitment either between God and humanity or among people. They are often used synonymously, but again, difference matters.

Covenant is found in a variety of circumstances in Scripture, most notably as the groups of writings known as the Old Covenant and New Covenant. When used in secular contexts,[2] *covenant* is typically applied to

---

2 According to *The Law Dictionary Featuring Black's Law Dictionary Free Online Legal Dictionary 2nd Ed.*, A covenant is "An agreement <u>convention</u>, or promise of two or more parties, by deed in writing, <u>signed, sealed, and delivered</u>, by which either of the parties pledges himself to the other that something is either done or shall be done, or stipulates for the truth of certain facts. Sabin v. Hamilton, 2 Ark. 490; Com. v. Robinson, 1 Watts (Pa.) 1G0; Kent v. Edmondston, 49 N. C. 529 (http://thelawdictionary.org/covenant/)." Definitions of legal covenants can also be accessed on this website.

land ownership and use (examples: covenant of warranty, covenant of restrictions, covenant of easement, covenant not to compete). Whereas *testament* is found in biblical contexts as well as synonymous for Old or New Covenant, we also find it in secular settings, particularly in court cases and last wills. Related words like *agreement* and *contract* are more typically seen as secular terms. Let's drill down a bit into these terms.

Promise

A little girl was shopping with her father early one evening. On their way to the grocery store, they passed a toy shop. A beautiful doll was displayed in the window and did not go unnoticed by the little girl. She stopped and pulled her daddy's hand to come look at the window. "Daddy, I would love to have that dolly."

"Oh sweetie, I know. I'll buy you that doll for your birthday that's coming up this Saturday." The little girl hugged her dad and they went on their way to the grocery store.

All week long at school, she told her friends, "Saturday's coming. My daddy is bringing me the doll I want. Saturday's coming." Saturday came and the so did the doll. The little girl knew her daddy so well that with unwavering confidence, she told everyone about the doll before it even arrived. She had no doubt because her daddy was a promise-keeper.

The point of the story is about keeping a promise. It does not necessarily demand anything from the recipient. It is not a contract and does not demand a signature. A promise is a declaration of assurance about something that is expected. It is simply giving your word on either providing or doing something.

A promise can be big. Giving a diamond ring for engagement is a token of promise to marry—that's really big considering it forecasts a lifetime commitment. A promise can also be small like promising to meet for coffee on Tuesday, although it can become big too if you show up an hour late or not at all. Promises lead the receiver to believe in something to come or expect the promise-maker to do what is pledged.

Moses led the Israelites to their future home called the Promised Land. God fulfilled that promise with some spectacular miracles. The incarnation of Jesus is the Promised Messiah, who came in the fullness of time. Before the ascension, Jesus told His disciples to wait in Jerusalem for the promise of the Holy Spirit, and they were all baptized in the Spirit on Pentecost. God always keeps His promises.

Keeping a promise has moral and ethical aspects—the promisor is expected to both know and do what is right following the example and imperatives of God's Word. The relational consequences of broken promises are loss of trust, reliability, and credibility on top of tangible losses in the case of goods and services.

A common misconception is that a verbal agreement—a hand-shake deal—is as good as a written contract. Not so—broken verbal agreements have no recourse or remedy in secular courts.[3] Verbal agreements may work among people of like-mindedness when it comes to keeping one's word, but as a societal value, it has seen much erosion. A broken verbal agreement may create cynicism and hurt on a personal level, but from a legal standpoint, a promise or agreement is not enforceable unless it had moved into a legal contract prior to the breach.

Agreement vs. Contract

Many years ago, my husband and I hired someone who was recommended by a friend to lay new floor tiles and install a pedestal sink in a bathroom next to our den. We purchased the necessary supplies. In good faith and with his verbal agreement to do the job well, we paid him for his labor. He made a complete mess. Everything he did had to be ripped out and done over. We had no recourse of compensation for the mess because we did not

---

[3] Disclaimer: This is a general knowledge description from a non-professional source available to the general public on the Internet. It is not intended or given as legal advice. Whenever you have legal issues or questions, most especially involving a legal transaction, it is always wise, prudent, and recommended to obtain advice and counsel from a legally qualified and certified attorney.

have a formal contract. The agreement was verbal and based on a handshake. Lesson learned.

Contract and agreement are related in that they involve two or more parties willing to do something for each other, but they are not the same thing. Two people can agree to do something or to exchange something, but that does not make it a contract. Simple agreement could mean people concurring on an opinion or it can involve them doing a favor for each other.

Verbal agreements express a desire or commitment, but they are not binding in an official sense. An agreement could be as simple as swapping comic books or as complicated as siblings deciding on how they will share the care of their elderly parents. An ethical or moral person would say an agreement should be kept, but in reality, it is not enforceable. It is dependent upon the individual's commitment to do what is morally and ethically right.

A contract is more than just a simple agreement. It differs from agreement in a fairly basic way. A verbal agreement is not legally enforceable, whereas a written contract is. Verbal agreements rely on the ethical and moral character of the parties involved, but have no recourse when the agreement is not fulfilled. Agreement is actually best understood as the path or prerequisite of contract or covenant.

An agreement becomes contractual when it is legally binding and enforceable, having the elements of a contract.[4] Four basic elements of a typical legally binding contract should include:

(5)
(1) a written offer (with time limitations)
(2) acceptance by the parties involved
(3) an intention of legal consequence if not upheld
(4) some form of consideration, whether monetary or other.

---

[4] Uslegal.com offers the following definition: "The requisite elements that must be established to demonstrate the **formation** of a **legally binding** contract are (1) offer; (2) **acceptance**; (3) **consideration**; (4) **mutuality** of obligation; (5) competency and capacity; and, in **certain circumstances**, (6) a **written instrument**." (US Legal, Inc., https://contracts.uslegal.com/elements-of-a-contract/, accessed May 31, 2017).

What makes a contract enforceable is when all parties (ones that are legally competent, capable, and of legal age to make agreements) are in agreement in writing; an exchange is made of something that has value (cash, goods, services, or a promise); and a signature (seal) of some kind bears witness to the agreement. Examples of where contracts are used include the purchase of real estate, hiring a company to do repairs on something, or hiring a company to perform a special service like photographing a wedding. Typically, contracts should have terms of resolution in cases of contract breach. We rely on contracts to hold parties accountable to the details to which they agree.

Testament and Covenant

Covenant and *testament* are used interchangeably when referring to biblical texts even though each has a unique focus as to content. Most people are comfortable with this. However, knowing the subtleties of how each adds meaning provides deeper appreciation for the wholeness of its contents.

How are testament and covenant different? Referring to them as *testaments*, the Old and New Testaments reveal the legacy and the terms to receive the inheritance God has for His people. Referring to them as *covenants*, the Old and New Covenants reveal the integrity of God's word to His people, and His character to faithfully execute that which He has covenanted. On the one hand, the difference may appear subtle, yet on the other hand, it impacts how we perceive and apply God's Word.

Testament

Testament can be found in both biblical and secular contexts. To testify means to speak as a witness to an event or truth. In the secular context of a legal last will and testament, the will confirms the true desire of the person (the testator) leaving the dissolution of worldly goods with the intent that those wishes are carried out to the letter. The word *testament* in biblical contexts actually carries a somewhat similar idea in that we are inheritors of God's promises.

Inheritance is a major theme in the Old Testament as revealed in God's promise to Abraham, and often reiterated.

> Remember Abraham, Isaac, and Israel, Your servants to whom You swore by Yourself, and said to them, 'I will multiply your descendants as the stars of the heavens, and all this land of which I have spoken I will give to your descendants, and they shall inherit *it* forever' (Ex 32:13).

Inheritance is also a major theme in the New Testament. As believers and followers of Jesus, we receive an inheritance of eternal life through the death and resurrection of Christ.

> For this reason He is the mediator of a new covenant, so that, since a death has taken place for the redemption of the transgressions that were *committed* under the first covenant, those who have been called may receive the promise of the eternal inheritance (Heb 9:15).

The Bible is the Word of God, inspired by the Holy Spirit for our edification, knowledge, and guidance. As a document of witness, the Bible also serves as a testimony of the character, nature, and works of God. Therefore, referring to these two collections of writings as testaments seems fitting.

COVENANT

Covenant in Hebrew is *bareeth*. It carries the concept of a compact or a league or confederacy. It is derived from *bara*, meaning to cut, to create, to make "fat" and *barah*, to eat. The cutting part is important as part of covenant-making in Old Testament terms. An example is found in Gn

15:9–10, where God makes a covenant with Abraham regarding the land and prophesies future enslavement and deliverance of his descendants. As directed, Abraham cut in two the animal parts as part of the blood sacrifice in the covenant making, and ". . . there appeared a smoking oven and a flaming torch which passed between these pieces" (Gn 15:17).

The word "covenant" used for the entire body of thirty-nine books of the Old Covenant is used as a holistic term.[5] It broadly reveals God's plans and purposes for all of humanity, and for Israel in particular. In the Israelite world before Christ, this body of biblical literature contained the core beliefs and guiding principles holding the Israelite people together as a nation under God's laws. To a large degree, the same can be said of Jews as a people group throughout the world today.

Like the Old Covenant, the word *covenant* is used in a broad and holistic sense as well. As a body of biblical literature consisting of twenty-seven books, the New Testament/Covenant contains the core beliefs and guiding principles holding followers of Christ, the children of God, together as a nation in the heavenly kingdom.

The Greek word for covenant is *diatheke*, referring to the disposition of a will or testament. It derives from *diathithemai*, meaning to dispose of or appoint as in a bequest. Here the focus shifts on fulfillment of the testator's (God) desires and will. The two terms, *covenant* and *testament* are

---

[5] The discussion of covenant in this and subsequent chapters is not intended as critique of traditional theological persuasions regarding biblical frameworks like Covenant Theology (sometimes referred to as Federal Theology, viewing the history of God's dealings with humanity through periods of a covenant of works and a covenant of grace), Wesleyan Covenant Theology (an Armenian adaptation of covenant theology in the area of soteriology), Dispensationalism (dividing history into seven periods of covenant relationship with God, a schematic developed by J. N. Darby in the nineteenth century), or more recent views (Eiben 1999, Gräbe 2002, Ruthven 2008) of covenant that have given fresh insight on the Holy Spirit and the gifts of the Spirit as pre-eminent in the fulfillment of promise in the New Covenant. These are systematic frameworks used to interpret overall biblical structure and message. They describe such themes as sin, redemption, relationship with God's plans and purposes, and the consummation of the ages. The explanation and narratives of covenant in this chapter and subsequent ones are about the meaning and elements of covenant as a form of agreement and promise, mostly between God and humanity, both individually and collectively.

used as synonyms for the New Testament/Covenant, but as with the Old, the emphasis makes a subtle difference in perspective.

TERMS: READ THE SMALL PRINT

Contracts and covenants have terms (details), a mediator, and a signature/seal. Terms are the limiting factors, the provisions and details of the agreement. It describes what is at stake, what the contractual agreement is about, and the specific recourse if broken.

The contract or covenant can be unilateral or bilateral. Unilateral covenants are ones where the covenant maker states what is promised, gives the terms of the covenant, but does not require the second party to do anything to receive what the covenant promises. Bilateral covenants are ones where both parties declare their promise, give the terms of the covenant, and each of the parties commit themselves to fulfill their part.

A covenant can be eternal or temporal. This has to do with the time commitment of the covenant. The terms of the eternal ones do not stop. Eternal means forever. Temporal ones have either a specific time of fulfillment or have a specific event that fulfills the covenant, and then it is terminated. The fulfillment ends the commitment.

The terms are the details that spell out the purpose and process that is expected during the lifetime of the contract or covenant. The terms can be conditional, ("if . . . then . . ."). Terms can also be contingent about time, giving it a time frame to the cause and effect statement ("when . . . then . . ."). Terms are important because they describe the expectations and also the consequences of breaking the contract or covenant.

The terms of ancient covenants were typically recorded and preserved in an official manner. The huge cache of Hittite and Mesopotamian cuneiform tablets and ancient Egyptian papyrus documents, attest to the need for writing and preserving covenants for millennia. Now we record deeds in government record bureaus and keep official contractual documents for the life of its terms. When disputes arise, we refer back to the terms in the original documents as the defining test of a settlement.

Prior to Moses, the covenants between God and humanity appear to have been passed on verbally and then written down during the times of the Exodus. Archaeological evidence and intra-scriptural references for covenant writings prior to the Israelite Exodus appears to be lacking. While scholars disagree as to the authorship of the Torah (first five books of the Bible, also called Pentateuch), Scripture affirms that Moses had a hand in its writing (Ex 7:14, 24:4, 34:27; Lv 1:1, 6:8; Dt 31:9, 24–26; Jo 8: 31–34; 2 Chr 34:14).

Others who were called upon by the Holy Spirit to write the oracles of God added to the writings of Moses to form the canon of the Bible. Scripture reveals the person and work of God and reminds us of the terms of covenants between God and humanity. We rely on the authority and veracity of the Bible in the fulfillment of past covenants as we stand believing the new one.

MEDIATOR

A mediator is basically a broker. The mediator of a contract or covenant is the one who makes the contract or covenant possible; the one who negotiates the terms. It is often the one responsible for the outcome, a dispute settler. The mediator can be a broker, counselor, agent, liaison, proxy, or judge. The parties involved in contracts or covenants can also come to terms without a third-party mediator, especially in unilateral covenants, thereby serving as their own mediators.

In the ancient Israelite world, the concept of *goel*, meaning kinsman-redeemer, is an important role found in Scripture. The role of a *goel* is as a mediator, an essential person in Old Testament stories of covenants between people. Someone in the family, usually an uncle, brother, or sometimes a highly-valued servant, serves as the family kinsman-redeemer. An example of a *goel* is the servant who arranged the marriage of Isaac and Rachel.

In this family role of kinsman-redeemer, he can be the mediator in any of these situations:

- Being the blood-avenger who avenges a murder or a wrong done to a family member (Nm 35:9–34; Nm 5:8).
- Rescue a family member in trouble (Gn 48:16; Ex 6:6).
- Recover property or people in need of redemption (Lv. 27:9–25; Lv. 25:47–55).
- Mediate covenants and arranges marriages (Isaac and Rachel, Boaz and Ruth).

God is a mediator, promisor, and testator of His covenants to His people. As the *goel* to Israel, God redeemed them and their land time and again. Jesus is our *goel*, redeeming us from the curse of the law (Gal 3:13). "For there is one God, *and* one mediator also between God and men, *the* man Christ Jesus (1 Tim 2:5)." Hebrews 8:6, 9:15, and 12:24 identify Jesus as the mediator of a new and better covenant.

How is the New Covenant better? Does that mean former covenants were not up to par? Some treat the Old Covenant as inferior, as if it is the concoction of fearful men in the wilderness. If a perfect and good God gave the Law (Torah), wouldn't it be good? Didn't it serve well for its intent? Nothing that God does is inferior. The Torah fulfilled its divine purpose to the extent that it held Israel as a unified nation carrying the promise of Messiah. The Law served well as a tutor until the incarnation of Jesus Christ leading to faith in Him (Gal 3:24). It also served well to show us that we cannot achieve righteousness by works alone; it is a faith issue.

Some people dismiss the importance of the Old Covenant as virtually irrelevant, yet surely there is wisdom we miss if we solely focus on New Testament writings. The Gospels, Acts, and Epistles make repeated references to Old Testament truths. "For whatever was written in earlier times was written for our instruction, so that through perseverance and the encouragement of the Scriptures we might have hope" (Rom 15:4).

As New Covenant believers, we have God's law written in our hearts, but that does not mean we can dismiss the Old Covenant as having no part in our Christian walk and understanding of God. Whereas I am not suggesting that Christians are required to follow the many laws of Leviticus and Deuteronomy, particularly in light of Jesus' fulfillment, I am, however, proposing that the Old Covenant holds divine principles, examples, and understanding worthy of consideration and wisdom for all generations. It contains prophecy fulfilled in Christ and prophecy yet to be fulfilled.

The New Covenant is better (Heb 8:6), but not because the Old was deficient. In fact, the Old was perfect for its purpose, given by a perfect God for His perfect purposes. The first became obsolete because the mediator of the new (Jesus) fulfilled it and established the second (Heb 10:9). The New Covenant is better because it is the final and complete one enacted on better promises. It is the fulfillment of prophecy regarding the coming of Messiah, not needing anything more for humanity's redemption, and the hope of things to come (Heb 9:12).

The New Covenant moves us into a restorative relationship with God that was lost in Eden. God now writes His law on hearts instead of stone tablets.

> For all who have sinned without the Law will also perish without the Law, and all who have sinned under the Law will be judged by the Law; for *it is* not the hearers of the Law *who* are just before God, but the doers of the Law will be justified. For when Gentiles who do not have the Law do instinctively the things of the Law, these, not having the Law, are a law to themselves, in that they show the work of the Law written in their hearts, their conscience bearing witness and their thoughts alternately accusing or else defending them, on the day when, according to my gospel, God will judge the secrets of men through Christ Jesus (Rom 2:12–15).

This New Covenant is inclusive and satisfies the past, present, future, and eternity—completely reliable and enforceable by God.

Signed and Sealed

The signing of a contract is the obligation to fulfill the terms of agreement. It assumes that the signer is of legal age and mental condition to engage in such an agreement, as well as any other stipulated conditions within the contract. It also assumes that the signature is authentic and proof of the intent to execute the terms.

Before hand-written signatures of names were used to confirm a document, signet rings, stamp seals, and cylinder seals were used in antiquity to authenticate contracts, covenants, and testaments. In the ancient world, contracts were written on clay tablets. The signature stamp was impressed or the cylinder seal was rolled into wet clay to serve as agreement authentication, a signature of the owner. Cylinder seals are particularly interesting in that they are shaped like a bead. They were strung on cord or leather and worn like a necklace.

Signet rings have personal iconography (symbol, crest, initials) to indicate the identity of the owner. Official signature stamps were also used. In medieval times, wax was melted on to the parchment documents. The ring or stamp was impressed into the hot wax to authenticate the legitimacy of the document.

Signature stamps and corporate seals, although no longer in wax, are still used to verify legal documents. Modern corporations and notary publics use seals to authenticate official documents. Their use of seals has its origin in signature stamps used by kings and government officials long ago.

The whole point of these devices was to assure the identity of the ones who enter into the contractual agreement. Does God need a signature? "For when God made the promise to Abraham, since He could swear by no one greater, He swore by Himself," (Heb 6:13). God is the author of all creation. God is immutable, omnipotent, omniscient, and omnipresent. Who would have the audacity to challenge His word? His word is sufficient, but for the sake of humanity, God frequently provided signatures (seals) of His covenant, more as a reminder of His promises than an authentication of them.

The rainbow is the seal of the Noahic covenant (Gn 9:12–17). Circumcision was the seal of the Abrahamic covenant (Gn 17:11). The Holy Spirit is the seal upon the New Testament believer. "In Him, you also, after listening to the message of truth, the gospel of your salvation—having also believed, you were sealed in Him with the Holy Spirit of promise" (Eph 1:13). These seals, God's signature, serve as reminders of God's promises and blessings.

In a broad sense, The Old and New Testaments are covenants between God and humanity that carry the weight of God's attributes (immutability, omnipotence, omniscience, and omnipresence[6]). They attest to the inheritance believers receive as children of the Most High God. As a body of spiritual God-inspired writing, Scripture offers deep wisdom about what it means to be in covenant with God, and by extension, models of covenant relationships among people.

Scripture is also the declaration of God's will towards humanity that is firm, unshakable, and perfectly trustworthy. God's Testaments focus on bearing witness of Himself and assurances of His promises. The Old Testament bears witness to God and His relationship to people before the birth of Christ, and the promise of Messiah; whereas New Testament focuses on the witness of Jesus and Holy Spirit in His followers as inheritors of the promise.

The benchmark between Old and New Testaments or Covenants is the birth of Jesus. Should New Testament followers of Jesus dismiss the Old Testament as a dispensation over and done? The Old Testament stories are largely about the Israelites, God's chosen carriers of the Promise, and their history with God, but not entirely. Furthermore, even the stories involving Israel are for the instruction of all people. If we think of the Old Testament only or uniquely as a Jewish document, we deceive ourselves. All of Scripture is for all peoples.

"All Scripture is inspired by God and profitable for teaching, for reproof, for correction, for training in righteousness (2 Tim 3:16)." The

---

6 Immutability means the quality of being unchangeable. Omnipotence means all powerful. Omniscience means all-knowing. Omnipresence means present everywhere.

phrase God-inspired in Greek is *theopneustos*, meaning "divinely breathed in" and is translated as "God-breathed" in the New International Version. If we believe that Scripture is "God-inspired-divinely-breathed-in," we are compelled to mine all of it—Old and New Covenants—for His wisdom, apocalyptic revelation of things still to come, and insight for righteous living.

Understanding of covenants helps us to locate where we are in the scheme of history with God. It explains how we got here, where we are going, and why we are going there. The eighth through tenth chapters of Hebrews and the third chapter of Galatians illuminate the New Covenant terms for both the Jewish world that had centuries of history with the covenant-making God, and the Gentile world that was clueless as to the ways of God's covenant.

> Gentiles were excluded from the covenant of promise having no hope and without God. Jesus is our peace, making Jew and Gentile into one people, breaking down the barrier by abolishing the Law of commandments in ordinances, making the two into one man, reconciling both into one body through the Cross, putting to death the enmity. We are no longer strangers but are of one household of God (Eph 2:12–16).

The state of affairs at the point where Jesus arrives and completes His mission as the Son of Man is good news. He offers a new deal for both Jew and Gentile.

How was righteousness imputed before the Cross? A huge key about how God imputes righteousness is in Gn 15:6 and reaffirmed in Gal 3:6. "Then he [Abraham] believed in the LORD; and He [God] reckoned it to him [Abraham] as righteousness" (Gn 15:6, bracketed names added). This is worth highlighting in your Bible. The basis of all relationship with God is faith, not works (Gal 2:16). The blessings of Abraham came to Gentiles, ". . . so that we might receive the promise of the Spirit through faith" (Gal 3:14).

If it is by faith that we are made righteous, what was the point of the Law (works) in the Old Covenant? It surely was not capricious to expect people to keep 613 laws as a measure of righteousness. The Law was given because of sin – to harness sinful behavior until the promised seed comes (Gal 3:19).[7] If a law could make us righteous, we would not need a mediator; we would not need a Messiah, and the promise would be unnecessary, null and void.

The eighth chapter of Hebrews compares the Old and New Covenants and goes to the heart of the matter. Old Covenant priests and law are a copy and shadow of heavenly things, but Jesus is the mediator of a better covenant enacted on better promises (Heb 8:5–6). Old Covenant high priests were appointed to offer gifts and sacrifices in the earthly Temple, but Jesus is the high priest and minister in the heavenly true tabernacle (Heb 8:1–2) and offers His blood once and for all. Furthermore, if the first covenant had been complete and final, we would not need a second.

The Old Covenant ritual had to be repeated for national cleansing every year[8] because the blood of animals was not eternal or perfect. The New Covenant made the Old Covenant obsolete, not irrelevant or bad (Heb 8:13), being fulfilled in Christ. The purpose of the Blood of Christ as sacrificial, is that it cleanses our conscience from dead works (Heb 9:14). This is why Jesus is the mediator of a better covenant.

In the Old Covenant, death must take place for cleansing. The animals were a temporary and symbolic means of cleansing, but the one who made the covenant (God) required sinless, blameless, perfect blood to make it eternally valid and it required a death (Heb 9:16–18). Blood was always required for the forgiveness of sin (Heb 9:18–23), but animal sacrifice was a merely copy of the heavenly things. The real one is always better—Jesus (Heb 9:23–24). Judgment fell once and for all through Jesus,

---

[7] The Law helped to sustain Israel as a unique nation dedicated to the worship of Yahweh. It provided for ritual cleansing in the form of sin offerings for individuals and as national cleansing on *Yom Kippur* (Day of Atonement).

[8] The feast of *Yom Kippur* (Day of Atonement) is an annual event in the Jewish calendar that is specifically for ceremonial national cleansing (Lv 16:1–34, 23:26–32).

but He will ". . . appear a second time for salvation without reference to sin, to those who eagerly await Him" (Heb 9:27–28).

Hebrews 10:1–10 states that the Law only had a shadow of good things, otherwise it would not have needed to be continuously repeated. The first covenant must end in fulfillment for the second to come. We were kept "in custody" under law serving as a tutor that leads us to Christ so we may be justified by faith. Because of faith in Christ, we no longer need custodial care. We are sons of God through faith in Jesus and heirs of the promise (Gal 3:22-26).

This, then, is the New Covenant: ". . . I will put my laws upon their heart, and upon their mind I will write them (Heb 10:16b)" in fulfillment of Jer 31:33. In this new covenant, we have access to hear directly from God by the Spirit in the various ways He speaks and then we obey His voice. His law—what is righteous and godly—is written in our hearts.

We have assurance by faith in this New Covenant. "Hold fast the confession of our hope without wavering for He who promised is faithful" (Heb 10:23). Faith, then, is essential in the Christian life. Hebrews 11:1 defines faith as "the assurance [pledge, guarantee] of what is hoped for [all that Scripture promises, salvation, abundant life, and eternal life–the blessed hope], and the conviction [evidence] of things not seen" (bracketed words added). Faith reaches, propels, and sustains us in the direction of hope when things are not visible or tangible.

The Good News

In the creation, God created male and female in His image and blessed them (Gn 1:27) way before the fall. His Word of blessing cannot return to Him void (Is 55:1) and so He established covenants with humanity. He engaged directly with the likes of Adam, Noah, Abrahams, and Moses, all leading to the restoration of humanity to Himself because of His great love. God's character is revealed as utterly dependable. His Word is sure. We simply need to believe His Word to receive all that He has done and will do on our behalf.

Faith grows and increases as we continuously hear the Word of God (Rom 10:17). We develop a history with God as we get to know Him in His Word and in fellowship with Him. Our history with God becomes a powerful testimony, and propels our faith to believe God further. As followers of God, our desire is to please Him. All that we have in the here and now, and the destination of where we step into eternity, is appropriated by faith in God and His word. It is faith that reassures and holds us steady in times of distress, trials, and temptation, as we persevere to the end. And yes, faith pleases God.

PRAYER
Almighty God, You love humanity with such a great love that You have provided a new covenant through the finished work of Jesus whereby You enter into direct family relationship with those who believe You. I believe in the finished work of Jesus on my behalf and receive the forgiveness of sin He provided through His death and resurrection. I am now in your family. Thank you for such lovingkindness. Thank you, Holy Spirit, for Your presence and guidance in revealing Your will to me. Help me, Lord, to cherish Your covenant and to enter into a deeper communion with You, I pray in Jesus' Name.

GUIDE: QUESTIONS FOR DISCUSSION OR JOURNALING

Chapter Two: Unravel the "Legalese"

1. Which Old Testament covenants are still in effect? Why do you think God made these without at time or event endings?
2. Are the New Covenant terms only for believers or for the entire world?
3. What is the impact of understanding the terms of the New Covenant for believers?
4. How do you see the connection between the death, burial, and resurrection of Jesus and the terms of the New Covenant?

NOTES

NOTES

The Power of Covenant Words

When I was about ten years old I wanted a pair of street roller skates. They were the two-front-and-two-back-wheel kind that you attached onto your shoes and tightened with a skate key. It was a big deal to me because I rarely asked for toys. My mom promised to buy them. My skinned knees from learning how to skate attested to Mom's follow-through to purchase.

I mention this because of my mother's character in giving her word. She never made casual promises that might not be kept. When she said "yes" to something, it was as good as done. The same was true for a "no." Her honesty and integrity were at stake, and she refused to compromise it. Her attitude about keeping her word modeled integrity for me.

Jesus had something to say about the giving of one's word on matters of personal relationships.

> But I say to you, make no oath at all, either by heaven, for it is the throne of God, or by the earth, for it is the footstool of His feet, or by Jerusalem, for it is the city of the great King. Nor shall you make an oath by your head, for you cannot make one hair white or black. But let your statement be, 'Yes, yes' *or* 'No, no'; anything beyond these is of evil (Mt 5:34–36).

Jesus makes the point that swearing oaths, vows, or promises by holy or irrefutable things to back it up are unnecessary if the person's word is their bond. Needing to swear beyond one's word implies that the promisor and the promise are potentially unreliable.

The trustworthiness of promises and integrity of promise makers are at stake. Warning: Commitments may mean refraining from overspending, paying bills on time, sitting through boring events when attendance was promised, conducting reliable business deals, praying for those to whom prayer was promised, or following through on a multitude of casual interactions where a word is given.

The righteous ". . . swears to his own hurt and does not change. . ." (Ps 15:4b). Swearing to your own hurt means that even when it may cost you more than you thought or planned, your sworn word must have reliability. Integrity is the basis of trust among people and we have God's affirmation as we walk in it. "As for me, You uphold me in my integrity, And You set me in Your presence forever" (Ps 41:12).

We save the sweet, the finest, or the loveliest as the crème de la crème to highlight special moments. We understand the special nature of dessert, fireworks, and beautifully wrapped gifts. I like to think that it is God's design to do that. The crown of creation was God's reservation for the final of the six days of the creation of the world and everything in it.[9] Humans were the last and they were given dominion over all that came into being before them. They were the only ones created in God's image.

> Then God said, "Let Us make man in Our image, according to Our likeness; and let them rule over the fish of the sea and over the birds of the sky and over the cattle and over all the earth, and over every creeping thing that creeps on the earth." God created man in His own image, in the image of God He created him; male and female He created them (Gn. 1:26–27).

---

9 The literal six-day theory holds that God created the world in six twenty-four-hour days. The day-age theory holds that God created the world in six ages of undetermined length of time. Both theories hinge on the interpretation of the Hebrew word for day—*yom*, a word indicating time. It can mean a twenty-four-hour period; an unspecified period of time, season, or era; or even a specific day as when Scripture states "in the day of the Lord" or "in that day." Neither of these two theories changes the sequence of things created in the first chapter of Genesis.

Adam and Eve were created as triune beings having spirit, soul, and body, just as God is a triune being—Father, Son, Holy Spirit. To be clear and to emphasize, even though humans may be triune in nature, humans are not God, nor gods. God created them, forever distinct. God is the uncreated and eternal Being, holy and unlike any other.

The Trinity in the Godhead is expressed in Gn 1:26. The Hebrew word for God is *Elohim*, a plural and masculine form. Furthermore, the "us" in "Let us," is also plural, yet God is One. "Hear O Israel: The Lord our God is one Lord" (Dt 6:4). In this verse, the Hebrew word for God is also *Elohim*, a plural form. The concept of Trinity (three persons in one God) is virtually impossible to fully comprehend by our finite human minds in spite of attempts by the best of theologians, but Scripture supports it and we receive it by faith. Really, how can the created one fully comprehend the Creator? The tri-unity of humans—spirit, soul, body—albeit complicated, is far easier to comprehend.

Two Trees, Two People, Two Options

Two special trees in Eden among the many fruitful trees are central to God's first covenant.

> Then the LORD God took the man and put him into the garden of Eden to cultivate it and keep it. The LORD God commanded the man, saying, "From any tree of the garden you may eat freely; but from the tree of the knowledge of good and evil you shall not eat, for in the day that you eat from it you will surely die." (Gn 2:15–17).

The beauty and provision of the garden was fully available to Adam and Eve. They had unlimited access and communication with God, not having to perform ceremonial sacrifice as was the case after the expulsion from Eden.

God's unilateral covenant (a one-sided action without the agreement of the other) with Adam and Eve was simply stated. Do not eat of the one tree (the tree of the knowledge of good and evil).[10] God went so far as to forewarn that if they did, it would result in death. The covenant was simple—eat of any tree and enjoy Eden (the Tree of Life); eat of the one forbidden tree and experience death. It was not a complicated covenant.

The Tree of Life offered endless communion with the Living God and all the fullness entailed in that relationship. The Tree of the Knowledge of Good and Evil (antonymic pairs)[11] offered the sum total of moral and immoral knowledge, but is not life-giving, much like what humanism offers.

Adam and Eve had the choice of two options—to obey or disobey. Free will was a gift to humanity from the moment of creation. We can freely choose to love God above all else without compulsion. Some argue that Adam and Eve could not have had a full understanding of death since they had not seen or experienced it. However, it would be unjust of God to expect humans to do something they did not have the capacity to do. Adam and Eve had to have understood the concept of death—ultimate separation from physical life as well as its spiritual consequences in separation from God—for it to be meaningful for them and, more importantly, to be held accountable for it. One does not have to experience death to know about it. They chose rebellion.

In their betrayal of the creation covenant, they obeyed a voice other than that of God (Gn 3:6). In esteeming the voice of the deceiver above the voice of God, doubting His Word, and then acting upon the temptation,

---

10 Revelation 22:2 speaks of a tree of life in describing the new Jerusalem. "In the midst of the street of it, and on either side of the river, was there the tree of life, which bare twelve manner of fruits, and yielded her fruit every month: and the leaves of the tree were for the healing of the nations." It says twelve kinds of fruit at all times, not one a month. The number twelve appears as significant in 187 places in the Bible, twelve being a number of completion, particularly in governmental structure. Here are some examples: Israel had twelve tribes; twelve kinds of animal sacrifices are described; Aaron's ephod had twelve stones; twelve spies went into the Promised Land; Jesus was twelve when he amazed the leaders at the Temple; Jesus called twelve apostles; double twelve (twenty-four) elders sit round about the throne of God.

11 Antonymic pairs are opposites that seem to go together. They can be gradable (examples: young and old; full and empty); complementary (examples: day and night; alive and dead); or relational (examples: husband and wife; teacher and student). They are most often used as figurative language to make a salient point.

their disobedience amounted to idolatry, the sin that separates humanity from God. It is the prime directive that is repeated throughout the Bible having to do with the relationship with God (the first commandment of the ten given to Moses—Ex 20:3—and the first of the two given by Jesus—Mt 22:37). Even so, the most merciful and loving God did not end the story of humanity at the expulsion of His creation from Eden. Instead, God provided for redemption and return to relationship, but the redemption would be costly.

The consequence of Adam and Eve's betrayal, expulsion to the world beyond Eden, was just and merciful at the same time. The angels assigned to guard access to the Tree of Life in Eden (Gn 2:22–24) protected Adam and Eve from living eternally in the condition of death, that is, separation from God. They were consigned to the world beyond Eden as the consequence of their betrayal, a harsh world by comparison, wherein they would experience final separation from this world in physical death.

God's declaration of justice for sin was also accompanied with the promise of redemption. The judgment on the enemy was,

> And I will put enmity
> Between you and the woman,
> And between your seed and her seed;
> He shall bruise you on the head,
> and you shall bruise him on the heel (Gn 3:15).

This was the *protoevangelium*, the first good news. God's avowal was a unilateral covenant (a one-way promise) that carried no contingencies, no options, and no alternatives. It was just like the unilateral covenant concerning the two trees. It had to come to pass.

As when God spoke the world into existence, His Word on this judgment and promise of redemption was unshakable, and carried final authority with absolutely no possibility of reversals. In the fullness of time, God was faithful to fulfill His Word in the incarnation of Jesus, His passion, death, and resurrection. It was a costly promise and complete redemption.

BLOOD COVERING

Adam and Eve covered their nakedness with leaves, but God covered their nakedness with skins, which required the death of a living creature (Gn 3:21). It was the first blood sacrifice that acted as a covering for their bodies and covering for their sin. It was the first blood covenant and became the model for future blood covenants. It is at the center of the sacrificial ritual of *Yom Kippur* (Day of Atonement) involving sprinkling of the blood on the mercy seat in the wilderness tabernacle and during the first and second Temple periods (Lv 16).

Why blood? Simply stated, the covering of blood was a sacrifice of a life for the life of another. Blood carries oxygen and nutrients to the whole body. It removes waste and provides immunity from disease. The natural properties of blood (vasoconstriction, platelets, clotting proteins) are essential to healing wounds. It also binds all of humanity into one family, having DNA uniquely apart from other species.

It is not a stretch to see that in a like manner, it is symbolic of what God has done in the sacrifice of Jesus. In the final offering of the Blood of Jesus, humanity has the restoration of the Eden kind of relationship; the provision of spiritual nutrition to the Body of Christ; removal of the sin that that wastes away the spirit; and finally, the provision of *shalom*—wholeness to humanity in spirit, soul, and body. First John 2:2 states, "and He Himself is the propitiation [reconciliation, mediation, restoration] for our sins; and not for ours only, but also for *those of* the whole world." Furthermore, 1 Jn 4:10 states, "In this is love, not that we loved God, but that He loved us and sent His Son *to be* the propitiation for our sins."

Fig leaves as well as all other vegetation have no blood. They were the inadequate covering choice of Adam and Eve. Fig leaves cannot give a life for a life. This was at the heart of the issue that arose with the sacrifices of Cain and Abel. Cain's sacrifice of vegetation was not after the pattern that God set forth. Abel's was blood sacrifice, acceptable to God. Cain could have acquired an animal. He could have bartered for one with Abel, but he chose to devalue and ignore the holiness of what God had designed.

When Cain's sacrifice was not acceptable, he was unrepentant (Gn 4:3–7). God gave Cain the opportunity to change his way of thinking and even warned him that his attitude of heart would produce ill effects. Instead of repentance, Cain buried offense in his heart and ended up committing the first fratricide (Gn 4:8). Like Cain, each person is responsible for the attitudes of his or her heart—to allow offense to produce anger, or to keep one's heart free from offense.

The result of Cain's sin was the destruction of what was once a productive living for Cain. The fruit of the ground no longer yielded to him. He became a nomad, living a life of vagrancy instead of agriculture (Gn 4:11–12). It is intriguing that his descendant Lamech committed murder twice and claimed even greater protection of God's vengeance (Gn 4:23).

All was not lost for humanity in the death of righteous Abel. Once more, God provided a righteous lineage in Seth to replace that of Abel. Seth was born to Adam and Eve after Cain was exiled to wandering (Gn 4:25). The Son of Righteousness, Jesus, came through Seth's lineage (Lk 3:38). The creation covenant remained in effect awaiting its fulfillment.

GOD'S WORD IS TRUSTWORTHY

It was no shock to God that Adam and Eve chose to rebel. God is omniscient. He knows everything—past, present, and future. One might ask why God allowed the fall of Adam and Eve to happen, as if God controlled their lives and decisions. Adam and Eve were given free will to choose the fruit from trees. They were fully forewarned of the consequences of their choices, both positive and negative. To the omniscient God, it was not a surprise that they rebelled, but God's foreknowledge did not eliminate their having a choice or the validity of the choice. It also did not eliminate the consequence of that choice.

The covenant of creation informs us that we have the option to have faith in God and choose righteousness. Self-imposed consequences are the outcome of the choice Adam and Eve made and also of the choices we make. God is not a master puppeteer dangling human being on the stage of life. Free will means that God knows what you will choose, but gives you the choice anyway.

However, God also does not leave humanity without hope, unlike those desperately seeking, yet ultimately failing, to save themselves or, even worse, deluding themselves to believe there is no heaven, hell, or eternity. He sends what I call "warnings on life's billboards" through His Word, prophetic experiences, people, or events (remember, God forewarned Adam and Eve). Even so, He does not interfere with the ultimate choice of whether to accept or reject Him in spite of the eternal consequences because He has given free will to humanity.

God's grace and mercy in the face of poor choices present themselves in response to prayer and repentance. His mercy is abundant in His plan of redemption for humanity, providing a Messiah for the sake of final atonement. "For there is one God, *and* one mediator also between God and men, *the* man Christ Jesus, who gave Himself as a ransom for all, the testimony *given* at the proper time (1 Tim 2:5–6)"; and "In this is love, not that we loved God, but that He loved us and sent His Son *to be* the propitiation for our sins (1 Jn 4:10)."

God set the world in motion with astonishing complexity. He has positioned humanity as the crown of His creation; giving humanity dominion and stewardship over the earth. When things went awry at the fall, God did not annihilate the world and everything in it. He had already spoken His Word over creation and declared that it was good before the creation of humans. Even when subsequent destruction occurred like the flood during Noah's day, God provided for the earth and its living creatures to survive and find a new beginning. Complete devastation could not occur because of God's fixed and expressed intention over His creation.

When God created humans, He blessed them (Gn 1:28). Here was the situation—what to do about humanity's wrong choice and betrayal. God had committed His covenant Word over all creation from the beginning and His Word never fails. If God had extinguished His creation because of human betrayal, it would have been a breach of His Word about what He blessed (Gn 1:28). Isaiah 40:8 states, "The grass withers, the flower fades, but the word of our God stands forever." Furthermore, Heb 11:3a states, "And He is the radiance of His glory and the exact representation of His nature, and upholds all things by the word of His power." The surety of the faithfulness of God's Word is utterly profound.

At the moment of humanity's rebellion, God already had a plan of redemption and spoke it into existence just as He spoke the universe into existence. God offered Himself, the Son as Jesus incarnate, to redeem what was lost (Gal 3:13; Gal 4:5; Ti 2:14). The time between the fall and the birth of Jesus was a time where humanity developed a history with God while awaiting the arrival of Messiah. That history was a complex cycle of obedience, then sin, then repentance and restoration, then sin again to repeat the cycle, again and again. In the fullness of time, Jesus, the Messiah, came according to the promise (Gal 4:4).

Humanity's Do-Over

Noah, ninth generation from Adam through the lineage of Seth, was a righteous man (Gn 6:9), but his world had degenerated into total depravity. "Then the LORD saw that the wickedness of man was great on the earth, and that every intent of the thoughts of his heart was only evil continually" (Gn 6:5). Humanity was utterly corrupt with no desire for repentance. God's decision for a "do-over" was made only after evil was thorough and continual. "God looked on the earth, and behold, it was corrupt; for all flesh had corrupted their way upon the earth" (Gn 6:12). All flesh—that really did mean all. Well, except for one—Noah and his immediate family.

God provided a restart for humanity that would preserve the earth and all living things. This new beginning was accompanied by another covenant, one that was in addition to His creation covenant, not a replacement. Noah heard God's voice and obeyed according to all that God told him to do. The safety of the ark for Noah, his family, and the animals, from a flood of epic proportions was his reward for obedience.

In Gn 6:18, God tells Noah that He is establishing His covenant with him and his family before the first two boards were attached in building the ark. "But I will establish My covenant with you; and you shall enter the ark—you and your sons and your wife, and your sons' wives with you" (Gn 6:18). God's hand of protection is over those who are obedient.

The covenant was twofold. First, God declared a unilateral covenant (one way promise; no agreement or requirement from the recipient) with the earth (Gn 8:21–22; Gn 9:10–12). Essentially, God promises to never again destroy the entire earth again by flood. Furthermore, "While the earth remains, Seed time and harvest, And cold and heat, And summer and winter, And day and night Shall not cease" (Gn 8:22).

The second part of the Noahic covenant is a bilateral (two-sided, mutual) one in which some terms are God's responsibility and others are Noah's and his descendants (Gn 9:9–17). Here are the conditions or terms of the covenant:

1. Noah was charged to be fruitful and multiply, repopulating the earth.
2. Noah and his descendants are given dominion over the earth and its living creatures, much like Adam and Eve were given dominion in Eden.
3. God gives all creatures, plant and animal, as food with one restriction. They were not permitted to eat it while still alive (flesh with the life thereof).
4. Murder is forbidden. Murder at the hand of "man" is punishable by death at the hand of man.[12] God will not intervene or directly render consequence as He did for Cain. The responsibility for justice is in the hands of humanity.
5. This covenant has no time limits or dissolution clause. It is in effect for as long as the earth exists.

---

12 Note the difference between murder and killing. They are not the same thing. Murder is always killing, but killing is not necessarily murder. The commandment in the Decalogue is "Thou shall not murder (Ex 20:13). Murder has evil and premeditated intent. Killing in battle context is not considered murder. Manslaughter, voluntary or involuntary, is killing without premeditated intent, falling into the category of accidental death even when it is a by-product of another type of criminal act. The American jurisprudence system has degrees of murder and manslaughter (first, second, or third based on evidence of felony, malice, intent, and premeditation), but these degrees are not found in Scripture.

Often called the Noahic Law, this covenant is the beginning of all law. It is in effect for all people (Jews and Gentiles) because Noah was the restart of humanity. It was a straightforward covenant—Noah was given all living things for dominion and food, but he must not eat living flesh or murder. In comparing it to the creation covenant, it is apparent that God is preempting another Cain-Abel situation. For the first time, capital punishment for murder is given acquiescence under the heavens.

Blood shedding is a critical issue in that even the provision for food requires the animal to be dead. The shedding of human blood for corresponding consequence—blood for blood now had divine permission. It is significant also in that the shedding of innocent blood of Messiah would be the defining moment of atonement for all of humanity—blood for blood.

The first act Noah made upon entering dry ground was to offer sacrifice to God. It was not a requirement of God's covenant; it was an act to express thanksgiving. The fact that Noah had communication with God, and obeyed God in the events that led up to the flood, implies that he had faith in God. God spoke to Noah, and Noah believed God before the first raindrop. Noah's faith in God's word sustained him during the many years of ridicule as he assembled the ark. His faith in the true God who always keeps His word would be passed on through his descendants that were spared destruction.

Rainbow Sign

Of all the possible signs of covenant, God chose to use rainwater in the sky. A rainbow is formed by light passing through rainwater. The raindrops act like a prism that separates the sun's white light into its colors. Different wavelengths of color bend at different angles when traveling through a medium like water and reflect off of the water droplets (reflection and refraction). The result is an arc of banded color in the sky. It was rainwater that destroyed the earth, but now serves as the sign of covenant to never again be totally destroyed by rainwater.

The rainbow is God's signature of the covenant. It still serves humanity to remind us of God's covenant.

> When the bow is in the cloud, then I will look upon it, to remember the everlasting covenant between God and every living creature of all flesh that is on the earth." And God said to Noah, "This is the sign of the covenant which I have established between Me and all flesh that is on the earth" (Gn 9:16–17).

This covenant extends beyond Noah and his immediate family. It includes all of humanity as well as all living things on earth.

Finding a rainbow after a rainfall is always a marvel and delight. A rare double rainbow is guaranteed multiple postings on social media sites. Besides religious contexts, rainbows are found in virtually all aspects of culture—art, music, science, literature, technology, business, and more. They are the source of wonder and symbolic of hope.

Signatures on documents like applications, checks, and purchase agreements become the confirmation that identifies who is accountable to its terms. Rainbows are like God writing His signature across the skies, reminding the world of His promise to the earth. As one of nature's most beautiful effects, a rainbow continues to remind the world of God's seal of His covenant agreement with the earth and all living things. It identifies God as the covenanter on a grand and majestic scale.

But Floods Still Happen

Hurricanes, typhoons, and tsunamis have caused massive flooding. Thousand were dispossessed from their homes during the Katrina and Sandy hurricanes. Super typhoon Haiyan, one of the strongest storms in recorded history, left at least 10,000 dead and massive destruction on Leyte Island in the Philippines. Do these flood events void God's Word? Although tragic, none of them wiped out the entire human population or that of the animals in their environs as the one Noah survived.

Surviving the flood is not the only point of the story.[13] Saving Noah was God keeping His redemptive word given after the fall. The earth and humanity had to continue even in its utter wickedness to the last righteous man on earth, and then had to be preserved until the Redeemer comes (Gn 3:15). The Messianic promise was given as divine prophetic declaration and it had to come to pass—no options, no wiggle room. The character and integrity of God's Word was at stake, and was also never at jeopardy or risk. God's word is sure, reliable, and utterly trustworthy. The Noahic covenant is no less trustworthy.

IT IS WRITTEN

The declared Word of God in the covenant of creation is the power that sustains the universe. Whatever God speaks must be. It is the absolute in all of creation.

Jesus is the perfect model of declaring the power of the Word of God. The testimony of Jesus coming out of the forty day fast in the wilderness is exemplary. Jesus was hungry. Upon being tempted to turn stones into bread, Jesus says, ". . . It is written, 'Man shall not live on bread alone, but on every word that proceeds out of the mouth of God.'" (Mt. 4:4). Jesus was certainly addressing the content of the temptation, but His statement far exceeds relief for an empty stomach. In effect, Jesus declared that sustaining life for humanity is dependent upon God's Word.

Thousands of years of history attest to the steadfast integrity of God's Word. As New Covenant believers, we continue our own history with God as we await the *perousia*, the second coming of Jesus. Believers stand firm on the unshakable faithfulness of God's covenant established in the Genesis creation and the promises of the New Jerusalem to come (Rev 21).

---

13 The flood narrative is told in Genesis, but is also the source of myth and legend among numerous ancient cultures throughout the world. Ancient flood stories can be found in several cultures including the following: the Gilgamesh epic of Mesopotamia; the ancient Greek Ogygian flood; Bergelmir in Norse mythology; the Manu and Matsya mythology of India; the Gun-yu mythology of China; the Thai Khum Borom myth; and the Filipino Igorot flood myth.

The certainty of God's Word on a matter that brings a blessing or curse is at the heart of covenanting, and can be the difference between existence and extinction. Such is the power of God's utterances (2 Cor 1:20).

Imagine for a moment that we have power in our words to create or destroy, to change our circumstances or the condition of someone else. Is it possible? As humans created in the image of God (Gn 1:27), our words do have power. We can bless or curse, lift another up or tear them down, bring life or rain death by our words. Proverbs 18:21 states, "Death and life are in the power of the tongue: and they that love it shall eat the fruit thereof." Furthermore, James 3:8–10 addresses this power so poignantly.

> But no one can tame the tongue; *it is* a restless evil *and* full of deadly poison. With it we bless *our* Lord and Father, and with it we curse men, who have been made in the likeness of God; from the same mouth come *both* blessing and cursing. My brethren, these things ought not to be this way (Jas 3:8-10).

The wounds of false accusation or verbal abuse cut deep into the soul AND wreak havoc in relationships. Repeated broken promises and lies have the same effect. As Jas 3:10 says, these things ought not to be, most especially among "brethren," meaning followers of God. Conversely, the value of words of encouragement in times of distress or the importance of verbal affirmations produces positive belief in self and favorable relationships with others. At their core, the words we speak are issues of the heart.

The principle of blessing and cursing is applicable to all human beings. The creation and the Noahic covenants were for all of humanity. Likewise, the power of words to bless or curse is a principle that works for believers and non-believers alike. "The good man out of the good treasure of his heart brings forth what is good; and the evil *man* out of the evil *treasure* brings forth what is evil; for his mouth speaks from that which fills his heart" (Lk 6:45).

The underlying message is that we must be mindful of the words we speak to one another and make every effort to fulfill the promises we make even when they are inconvenient.

The Good News

Proverbs 18:21 says, "Death and life are in the power of the tongue, And those who love it will eat its fruit." It is not a suggestion or a possibility. Words can bless or curse. They can bring healing or destruction, not only in the spiritual world, but also in the natural world.

Matthew 12:37 says, "For by your words you will be justified, and by your words you will be condemned." Our words reveal our character and so we can check ourselves by what we say and how we say them. The good news is that we can grow in grace and truth so that we can train our mouths to speak blessings instead of curses.

God spoke to Joshua before he led the Israelites into the campaign for the Promised Land and told him to continually meditate on His Word so that he would have success (Jo 1:8). Christian meditation is not emptying one's mind, but rather filling the mind with God's Word so that in the circumstances we face, God's Word comes forth in strength and in the power of the Holy Spirit to accomplish all that it says.

We also hear God's prophetic word as we enter into prayer and communion with Him. He reveals His Will and we receive in faith to obey. When it is God's Word, it always produces life and godliness in us.

Prayer

Thank you, God, that Your words bring life to me. Your Word brings truth and light into every situation. I rely on Your Word for wisdom and power for life and godliness. I hide Your Word in my heart so that I won't sin against You. Lord, I ask that you show me where I can encourage others by giving them Your Word.

GUIDE: QUESTIONS FOR DISCUSSION OR JOURNALING

Chapter Three: Power of Covenant Words

1. How have the words of others been instrumental in your life?
2. Remember and share a time when standing on God's Word for a situation was significant. What did you learn from it?
3. In what ways are words creative or destructive?
4. How does speaking God's Word in prayer make it effective?

NOTES

NOTES

Relational Covenants

—⚏—

Salt Covenant: What's a pretzel without salt?
PRETZELS AND CHIPS ARE JUST not the same without the salt—and who could eat just one. Cooking without salt is generally bland and needs a lot of help to make it flavorful. The origin of salt is from the Latin *solarius*, from which we get our word *salary*—ancient Roman soldiers were sometimes paid in salt. Because salt was considered valuable long ago, the phrase "to salt an account" means to add value to it. And regarding value, things in shops are for *sale*—for salt—better yet, sometimes on *sale*. An Old Salt is a seasoned sailor and salty language is witty and earthy, or even racy.

As a basic commodity, salt has many uses. Here are some salty facts:

- Salt purifies; it kills bacteria. Any beach goer who happens to have a cut knows the sting when you go swimming in the ocean, but isn't it amazing how much faster it heals. How about when you have a sore in your mouth or throat—the dentist tells you to gargle with salt water—nasty, but effective.
- Salt completes food. Salt makes it tasty and flavorful, but too much makes it inedible. "Can that which is unsavory be eaten without salt? or is there any taste in the white of an egg?" (Jb 6:6).
- Salt preserves food, as in salted fish and meats. This was particularly important before refrigeration was invented.
- Salt is something that your body cannot live without, but does not produce. It must be replenished regularly, but not necessarily with

sodium chloride (table salt). Salts occur naturally in vegetables, so like Mom said, "Eat your vegetables!" Putting too much added salt in the diet risks hypertension. Too much salt is considered unhealthy and may cause water retention.

- Salts are substances that have ionic bonds (electrostatic attraction between opposite charged ions), which means that salts are the strongest chemical bonds in nature. Table salt (NaCl – Sodium Chloride) is an example.
- When you reduce the water in the human body, what is left? Approximately 60% of the male adult is water, and females about 55% (women typically have more fat). The rest is made up of about 60 elements found on earth, which we consider to be essential salts. Indeed, we are the dust and salt of the earth and the substance of stars.
- Scattering salt on the land makes it infertile. In the ancient world, strewing salt on the earth meant cursing it and keeping it from being re-inhabited.
  - And Abimelech fought against the city all that day; and he took the city, and slew the people that was therein, and beat down the city, and sowed it with salt (Ju 9:45).
  - A fruitful land into a salt waste, Because of the wickedness of those who dwell in it (Ps 107:34).
  - "Therefore, as I live," declares the Lord of hosts, The God of Israel, "Surely Moab will be like Sodom And the sons of Ammon like Gomorrah— A place possessed by nettles and salt pits, And a perpetual desolation. The remnant of My people will plunder them And the remainder of My nation will inherit them" (Zep 2:9).
- People who live in an area where it snows enough to have roads salted know the corrosive effects that salt has on their vehicles. The run-off from the salt spreading also affects the environment. When salt seeps into the waterways, it seriously damages plant and animal life.

Although these facts may be fascinating in the natural world, God has spiritual realities about salt that parallels that of its natural attributes.

A Friendship Covenant

It was common knowledge among ancient Israelites that a salt covenant was one of friendship, a strong bond between two parties based on choice to be bound together. Just as salts are the strongest ionic bonds, salt covenants were strong bonds that held people together based on their will. The ancients may not have known about ionic bonds, but God certainly did, and He spoke of it in terms of relationship.

> All the offerings of the holy gifts, which the sons of Israel offer to the LORD, I have given to you and your sons and your daughters with you, as a perpetual allotment. It is an everlasting covenant of salt before the LORD to you and your descendants with you (Nm 18:19).

The relationship between God and David is renowned in Scripture. It can surely be said that David was a friend of God in the deepest sense to the degree that the kingship over Israel through the lineage of David was a salt covenant. "Do you not know that the LORD God of Israel gave the rule over Israel forever to David and his sons by a covenant of salt" (2 Chr 13:5)?

Salt covenants speak of completeness, not lacking anything, the promise of perpetual provision, and the preservation of the bloodline of David occupying the throne of Israel through which Jesus descended. A salt covenant is permanent and perpetual. Like the nature of salt, it speaks of

- God's faithfulness: God always fulfills His promises
- God's immutability: He does not change His nature or character.
- God's purity: God is holy.
- God's completeness: God is lacking nothing.
- God's covenants: God's safety, protection, and preservation of His people.

Jesus made a point of telling us to be salt, yes BE salt – not just USE salt. "You are the salt of the earth; but if the salt has become tasteless, how can it be made salty again? It is no longer good for anything, except to be thrown out and trampled under foot by men" (Mt 5:13). Furthermore, Mk 9:50 says, "Salt is good; but if the salt becomes unsalty, with what will you make it salty again? Have salt in yourselves, and be at peace with one another."

In these Scripture references, salt is a metaphor used to describe relationships. As disciples of Jesus, we have a salt covenant with Him for our safety, protection, completeness, health, provision, and purity. In the same way salt purifies, preserves, is necessary, and adds flavor, we are to be that for others in our relationships. As we keep ourselves salty with one another, it brings about peace and friendship. In Mt5:13, Jesus make an important point about when salt has value and when it doesn't. Salt is only valuable when it is flavorful. Without that element, it is utterly worthless. Likewise, when we add flavor to our relationships, it is valuable, but without this flavor (safety, protection, completeness, health, provision, and purity), the relationship is damaged and becomes toxic.

Jesus came and gave His life to become the path of peace between the Father and mankind. Colossians 1:19–23, Rom 5:10, and 2 Cor 5:18–20 tell us that God reconciled mankind to Himself through the death of Jesus and that He has given us the ministry of reconciliation to bring others to that peace. Jesus said in Mt 5:13 that we are to be salt to the world. We partner with God to bring the essential ingredients of righteousness, redemption, and eternal salvation to an unclean sin infected world lacking flavor or preservation. In being salty, we bring peace between unregenerate man and God and between one another.

Reconcile has two words in Greek. *Katallasso* means to change from enmity to friendship as in 2 Cor 5:18–20. It never indicates that God is being reconciled to people, but rather always that people are being reconciled to God. God is not the problem. The difference is important. God has always been faithful to His covenants, but humanity has been at enmity with God since the Garden of Eden. Nevertheless, through the sacrificed Lamb, Jesus, God's righteousness and mercy reconciled man to Himself. He has always been the place of refuge. God's love and mercy upon humanity has been so from the beginning and He has provided a series of covenants to draw us to Himself.

The other word for reconcile is *diallasso*. It indicates mutual hostility between people that becomes changed to friendship. An example is in Mt 5:24 where it states, "Leave your offering there before the altar and go; first be reconciled to your brother, and then come and present your offering." Here is the amazing good news. We have been given the ministry of reconciliation whereby we can broker (be an agent of) peace between humanity and God, as well as between people. Having "salt" within us, we should live in such a manner that people see God through our actions and words. "Let your speech always be with grace, as though seasoned with salt, so that you will know how you should respond to each person" (Col 4:5-6).

The way in which we conduct ourselves should reflect the grace of God, showing unmerited favor just as God does. In other words, we show favor whether or not they deserve it. That is how God is with us. We do not deserve His abundant grace, but He gives it anyway. We salt our relationships by acting graciously, giving unmerited favor, bringing reconciliation one to another and each one to God. In so doing, we represent a perfect, holy, wonderful, loving God, while ministering the understanding of truth that will set people free.

A Friend Closer than a Brother

It is often said that "blood is thicker than water," meaning blood relationships are stronger, but in reality, it is not always the case. Sibling rivalry generally resolves itself into adulthood, but what if it doesn't? And what about the "only child" who grows up without siblings? Special friendships in covenant can be even closer than family.

The expectation in families is that siblings should support and protect each other at all cost. It is the basis of clannish belonging and tribal law. Families getting along with each other is ideal, but the lack of brotherly love is the stuff of drama. Sibling rivalry is a classic theme found in literature (Kafka's *The Fratricide*), in Shakespeare plays (*As You Like It*, *King Lear*), in film (*The Godfather, Part II*), in opera (*Nabucco*), and even musical theater (*Joseph and the Amazing Technicolor Dreamcoat*).

Siblings gone bad in the Bible is iconic—Cain and Abel, Jacob and Esau, Joseph and his brothers. Sadly, the Cain and Abel conflict ended in death—the first biblical record of fratricide. Both Jacob and Joseph had sibling relationships fraught with difficulty, but they found a way to make peace with their siblings. We expect siblings to work through their differences and conflicts by virtue of them having the same lineage, but sometimes friends are better at it.

Friendship relationships are different from familial ones in that they are forged and sustained by choice, not blood or familial duty. Sibling relationships are fixed. One is either a relative or not, whereas the level of friendship can vary from loose acquaintance to friend-closer-than-a-brother bonds. It is based on choice and commitment. When betrayal in families happen, they are emotionally catastrophic. The same can be said of close friendships that end badly, however, with family ties, a broken bond profoundly affects other members of the family. Consequently, the urgency of restoration of family becomes more pressing.

"Dude, I got your back!"

Friendship is complicated. We may have difficulty defining it, but we know it when we see it. Special energy is exerted to form friendships. The saying, "A friend is someone who knows you—warts and all—but loves you anyway," rings true. Friendship, however, is more than simply tolerating one another's craziness. The bonds between people are formed by each person giving and receiving something needed or wanted—a place of confidentiality in soul-bearing, a sympathetic ear to unload burdens, a person to share special interests and events, someone with whom to enjoy laughter.

I have heard friendship defined in seasonal terms. Some are in your life for a short time, some for longer time, and a rare few for a lifetime. I have some friends that live far away. It may be months between contact, even brief ones. Yet when we meet, we pick up where we left off like no time has passed. Not an uncommon phenomenon. Each friend deposits something special, whether a short or long-term friendship.

Friendship is sometime separated into relationship categories like associate, acquaintance, "brother-from-another-mother," close friend, kindred spirit, bosom buddy. The closeness of friendship appears to be dependent on transparency and trust. A close friend should be one to whom you can trust with your deepest and even darkest secrets. This is risky business, and is why betrayals are so painful.

Friends can forge close lifelong relationships, as was the case of Jonathan and David. David was but a teenager when Samuel anointed him to be king over Israel. David did not take the throne immediately. He waited until Saul's death to ascend the throne, but the wait was fraught with conflict.

Saul's jealousy over David's success and popularity was such that he wanted David's death. A further complication for Saul was the deep friendship that Saul's son Jonathan had with David.

> Now it came about when he had finished speaking to Saul, that the soul of Jonathan was knit to the soul of David, and Jonathan loved him as himself. Saul took him that day and did not let him return to his father's house. Then Jonathan made a covenant with David because he loved him as himself. Jonathan stripped himself of the robe that was on him and gave it to David, with his armor, including his sword and his bow and his belt (1 Sm 18:1–4).

Jonathan's devotion to David was a covenant of brotherhood, much deeper than a casual friend relationship.[14] Jonathan made a unilateral covenant

---

14 The phrase "covenant of brotherhood" is mentioned in Am 1:9. It extended the idea of brotherhood to nations. "Thus says the Lord, 'For three transgressions of Tyre and for four I will not revoke its *punishment*, Because they delivered up an entire population to Edom, And did not remember *the* covenant of brotherhood' (Am 1:9)."

to protect and defend David. The seal of Jonathan's covenant was the gifts he gave to David—his robe, armor, sword, bow, and belt. These items were highly personal and represented the protection Jonathan was offering David.

Soon after Jonathan realized that Saul intended to kill David, Jonathan and David committed themselves to a covenant of protection and provision towards each other and their posterity. "Jonathan said to David, 'Go in safety, inasmuch as we have sworn to each other in the name of the Lord, saying, 'The Lord will be between me and you, and between my descendants and your descendants forever' (1 Sm 20:42)." Second Samuel tells the story of how David remembered and kept his covenant with Jonathan in showing kindness to Jonathan's lame son Mephibosheth after Jonathan's death (2 Sm 9:6–11).

God's Friends

Having a true friend in your lifetime is a treasure worth cherishing. I thought about the attributes of a true friend. Here are some qualities in a very practical way that would fit the description. A true friend is one who:

- Listens to your deep thoughts, opinions, events, concerns, and sadness with the stipulation that it won't be broadcast to the immediate world. Confidentiality matters.
- Likes being with you even when you are cranky.
- Is mindful of your circumstances—insists on sharing the check or offers to pay the whole thing when you need it.
- Offers to help you before you even ask.
- Can be counted upon to help out in a crisis—large and small.
- Gives you advice or opinions without insisting you follow it.
- Tells you the truth about how the outfit looks on you without making you feel stupid about selecting clothes that look horrible on you.

- Remembers the details—your birthday, your favorite dessert, music you like, and more.
- Knows when to laugh with you, when to hug, and when to cry with you.
- Finishes your sentences when words are at a loss.
- May not see you for long periods of time, but when you meet again, picks up the relationship as if no time has passed.
- Keeps promises.

If you find one or two friends like this in your lifetime, it is a treasure. "A man of *too many* friends *comes* to ruin, But there is a friend who sticks closer than a brother" (Prv 18:24).

James 2:23 says, "and the Scripture was fulfilled which says, 'And Abraham believed God, and it was reckoned to him as righteousness,' and he was called the friend of God." James is quoting the reckoning of Abraham as righteous by faith in in Genesis 15:6. Calling Abraham God's friend is found in 2 Chr 20:7, where it declares, "Did You not, O our God, drive out the inhabitants of this land before Your people Israel and give it to the descendants of Abraham Your friend forever?"

Moses was also a friend of God. "Thus the LORD used to speak to Moses face to face, just as a man speaks to his friend" (Ex 33:11a). Face to face implies the kind of intimacy close friends have. It's the kind of friendship where Moses could dialogue with God over his assignment to be the deliverer of his people. Later he was able to intercede on behalf of the Israelites in the wilderness when they were misbehaving.

What kind of friend was God to Abraham, Moses, and to all who believe in Him? Everything that God said He would do came to pass, bar none. "So will My word be which goes forth from My mouth; It will not return to Me empty, Without accomplishing what I desire, And without succeeding *in the matter* for which I sent it" (Is 55:11). His Word—God's promises and covenants—has complete reliability and credibility.

FRIEND AND BROTHER

Whom do we call friend—someone we just met; someone we know casually; someone we have known a long time? Short-term or casual acquaintances and lifelong friends seem to be lumped together in the one word—friend, yet clearly, we have a broad range of relationships. It takes a great deal of ebb and flow of situations before we determine their trustworthiness. That's how it is with people, but not with Jesus.

Jesus, our best model, had friends in Galilee and Judea—some closer than others. Jesus expressed the qualities of the salt of the earth to all whom He encountered—purifying, preserving, healing. He spent a lot of time with the twelve, but there were others in His sphere of influence. The seventy that Jesus sent out to minister (Lk 10) were close enough to be entrusted with the mission. The 120+ believers in the upper room awaiting the coming of the Holy Spirit on Pentecost (Acts 1:15) all knew Jesus and considered Him friend—certainly enough to obey His last words.

Jesus is the ultimate friend—one who really does stick closer than a brother and one who laid down His life for you. He fits every possible definition of what true friendship is supposed to be. "No longer do I call you slaves, for the slave does not know what his master is doing; but I have called you friends, for all things that I have heard from My Father I have made known to you" (Jn 15:15). Jesus extends his friendship to His followers and calls them brother. He said, "For whoever does the will of God, he is My brother and sister and mother" (Mk 3:35).

Jesus is both brother and friend to those who believe in Him. "Greater love has no one than this, that one lay down his life for his friends" (Jn 15:13). Jesus offers to the world the closer-than-a-brother kind of friendship that required the ultimate sacrifice on behalf of humanity—death on a cruel cross, resurrection from the dead, and ascension with the promise of return. The moment we come to Jesus and receive Him as Savior and Lord, He extends His eternal friendship, brotherhood, and eternal faithfulness.

He never abandons nor forsakes us (Heb 13:5). He gives life abundantly (Jn 10:10). He promises, "You did not choose Me but I chose you, and appointed you that you would go and bear fruit, and *that* your fruit would remain, so that whatever you ask of the Father in My name He may give to you" (Jn 15:16). There is no greater friend than Jesus, and He bids us to be family and friend.

The Good News

The good news is that not everybody you know is your friend. That's not mean or bad. It's about wise perspective. Some people are acquaintances, some are colleagues, some are just familiar faces you encounter from time to time. Simply being pleasant and kind does not qualify as friendship, although it could be a start. Friendship requires time spent together in various contexts.

Like ants, humans are wired to be social creatures. We interpret withdrawal from social contact as emotional pain and unhealthy. The safety that hermits and loners seek in their self-exile is considered eccentric at best. Even so, some relationships—with friends or even relatives—are toxic and are probably best either terminated or distanced. Restoration that leads to healthy relationship is always preferred, but not always possible. That is reality, but when brokenness leads a person to be reclusive with all of society, the best of a good friend relationship—trust, acceptance, and love—is missing.

If you have had some shaky friendships that left you upset and leery about trusting again, the good news is that your emotions can be healed and you can find real friendship. It requires you to have a clear idea about the nature of friendship—what it means to both be and receive a friend that is healthy for you. The models of character—the fruit of the Spirit (Gal 5:22–23)—gives a good idea of what to look for in a friend and be the "salt" people need.

A solid friendship has a "give and take" quality whereby each person has the other's best interest in mind. It is one that is based on honor, honesty, and integrity.

Prayer

Heavenly Father, thank you for Your lovingkindness that never fails. Thank you, Jesus, for being a brother and a friend, always faithful and seeking the best for me. You gave Your life for me, the ultimate gift. Holy Spirit, I ask for Your help with discernment about relationships that bring You honor. Forgive me, Lord, for times when I have not been the kind of salt you describe in Your Word and I forgive those who have been unkind toward me. Help me to be salt to those I encounter—bringing truth, honesty, faithfulness, integrity, and healing—to every relationship. Thank you, Lord, that You provide all that I need for life and godliness. Help me to be the kind of friend to others that brings You glory, I pray in Jesus' Name.

GUIDE: QUESTIONS FOR DISCUSSION OR JOURNALING

―∞―

Chapter Four: Relational Covenants

1. Jesus said that we are to be the salt of the earth. What does that look like in the context of your community?
2. What are your thoughts about Rom 8:5 regarding adoption as children of God?

"For you have not received a spirit of slavery leading to fear again, but you have received a spirit of adoption as sons by which we cry out, "Abba! Father!" (Rom 8:15).

3. Can someone be a friend of God and not a child of God?
4. What character traits are most important in friendship?

NOTES

NOTES

Intimate Covenants

MANY YEARS AGO, MY HUSBAND and I were visiting a pastor and his wife in another state. As we were having dinner at a restaurant, a very attractive woman happened to pass by the restaurant. We would not have even noticed her, but the pastor was so focused on her that his head turned in her direction at the same pace as she walked. His wife noticed and poked him, waking him out of his reverie. She explained that the pastor had struggles "with his eyes." We didn't probe for more information, but they offered further explanation. They said that as a strategy, they agreed that the wife would hold her husband accountable whenever she noticed his eyes fixed on a woman. We were not sure what that accountability would entail as no further details were shared.

At first I thought it was pretty brave of the man to agree having his wife help him with his wandering eye problem. Kudos for that. Then it occurred to me that as a strategy, it did not solve the problem or transform the man. It only made his wife the gatekeeper of his weakness. What happens when wifey is not around? Real repentance means change—a transformation—with the empowerment of the Holy Spirit, not just sorrow for wrongdoing. It seemed like the couple's agreement amounted to no more than applying a band-aid where surgery was needed.

COVENANT WITH EYES: A STRATEGY FOR PURITY

Rarely the topic of Sunday morning's sermon, the discussion of "wandering eyes" is not comfortable, but so necessary. With the advances of electronic devices and lowering of media standards over the last fifty years, both soft and hard pornography has become much more available than in the past.[15] As a result, it requires diligence to resist lustful temptation. God's Word on the matter is quite plain. "For God has not called us for the purpose of impurity, but in sanctification. Consequently he who rejects this, is not rejecting man but the God who gives His Holy Spirit to you" (1 Thes 4:7–8).

Job speaks to the issue of wandering eyes in a somewhat startling way. Upon considering his integrity, Job says, "I have made a covenant with my eyes; How then could I gaze at a virgin" (Jb 31:1)? The statement implies that Job had to have come to terms with the issue in the past and made a firm decision to keep himself from indulging in unrighteousness. He had even set a strategy in place to keep himself accountable.

Job's words "covenant with my eyes," is not one we typically hear preached. By using the word covenant, Job is making a serious declaration with no holds barred. The terms of the covenant are startling.

> If my heart has been enticed by a woman,
> Or I have lurked at my neighbor's doorway,
> May my wife grind for another,
> And let others kneel down over her.
> For that would be a lustful crime;
> Moreover, it would be an iniquity *punishable by* judges.
> For it would be fire that consumes to Abaddon,
> And would uproot all my increase (Jb 31: 9–12).

Job is submitting himself and his wife to be cursed and victimized by the lust of another if he breaks covenant with his eyes. The severity of such a

---

15 According to the Barna Group, 77% of self-identified Christian men between the ages of eighteen and thirty view pornography at least once a month. Furthermore, 40% of married men view porn more than once a month and 35% have extra-marital affairs; 22% of married women view porn more than once a month and 17% have affairs. (American Family News Network, *One News Now*, https://www.onenewsnow.com/culture/2014/10/09/survey-alarming-rate-of-christian-men-look-at-porn-commit-adultery, accessed May 31, 2017).

curse does not imply he expects this to happen, but rather that it is such a serious matter that he made the ultimate "if . . . then" avowal. Job also declares that such iniquity is subject to eternal judgment that ends in fiery Abaddan (place of complete destruction, desolation, and death). It is the same consequence as Jesus spoke about in Mt 18:9, the fiery hell—pretty serious stuff.

Job's final covenant statement on the matter is that such evil would also affect his prosperity. He says in verse twelve that this sin uproots his increase. The connection between sexual sin and loss of prosperity is not for the next life; it is for the here and now. Job was not willing to risk the blessings of God for increase to accommodate lust. As a strategy for purity, Job made a covenant with himself (his eyes).

This begs the question, "Does sin in one area affect the blessing in another?" We look to Scripture to find exemplars in order to establish precedence or principle. God promises blessing when walking uprightly. A case in point is Abraham. In Gn 17:1–2, God tells Abraham, "Walk before me, and be blameless. And I will establish My covenant between Me and You. And I will multiply you exceedingly." Blamelessness is based on faith in God (Gn 15:6, Gal 3:6). Keeping yourself in faith positions you to receive all that God has for you. Conversely, keeping yourself in sin positions you to invite destruction (Jn 10:10). James 5 and 1 Jn 5 speak of the ultimate destruction of sinful living as opposed to the overcoming power in following God.

Job made a covenant with his eyes as a strategy for keeping himself pure to avoid the consequences of lust. Job's self-imposed covenant to control himself worked for him, but it was based in sin consciousness rather than God consciousness. There is no mention of doing what is right simply because it is the way of life to honor God. It was to avoid punishment. He was doing all of the right things, but his focus was just that—doing the right things out of his own knowledge of ethics and morality.

We can put controls into our lives and follow programs to overcome destructive behaviors. Not to minimize their efforts, programs and therapists do have some great success. They are admirable and laudable. Society is better for them. Even so, if they are solely works-based, an important piece is missing. In the last chapter, Job realizes his failure in his relationship with God as the core of his life and he repents (Jb 42:1–6). Here is where Job moved from sin consciousness to God consciousness.

The same conclusions are found in Ecclesiastes. In the beginning, Solomon says, "All things are wearisome; Man is not able to tell *it*. The eye is not satisfied with seeing, Nor is the ear filled with hearing" (Eccl 1: 8). Lust is never satisfied. It moves humanity from event to event, never having sustained fulfillment. The end of Ecclesiastes provides the simple truth and fix to live righteously—God conscious. "The conclusion, when all has been heard, *is*: fear God and keep His commandments, because this *applies to* every person. For God will bring every act to judgment, everything which is hidden, whether it is good or evil" (Eccl 12:13–14).

Jesus addresses this problem to married men (Mt 5:28), but the principle certainly applies to married women as well. In Mt 5:28, Jesus said, "but I say to you that everyone who looks at a woman with lust for her has already committed adultery with her in his heart." Jesus further instructs that if eyes or hands are the source of offense, pluck out eyes and cut off hands (Mt 18: 8–9). It is not difficult to understand that Jesus was speaking metaphorically, otherwise we would have a lot of maimed and blind people. The point is that we have the power and responsibility to monitor what we allow to occupy our attention and make a home in our minds. Those things that are ungodly need to be cut off, not only because of innate wickedness and consequence, but even more importantly, they dishonor the God of our confession of faith and the testimony of our walk with Him.

Jesus informs the hearer that the consequences of informed, intentional, and unrepentant sin is fiery hell (Mt 18: 9). It may not be a popular topic, but hell is real. Humans may not have been intended to populate it, but by not choosing God, their own unrepentant dark hearts in rebellion to God will lead them there. God gives enough warnings and guidance in tandem with love, grace, and forgiveness for anyone to be free from the path to perdition, but we must receive His grace by faith (Jn 3:16–21).

Adultery does not begin in the bedroom; it finds fulfillment there. Nobody wakes up one morning and says, "I think I'll commit adultery today." The same can be said of other sins. It begins with a thought in the mind—a temptation. Instead of getting rid of the thought immediately, it is allowed to take up residence. That allows the temptation to take a beachhead, and then form a stronghold. Corresponding action soon follows.

The battleground for righteous living and a transformed life is in the mind—from a former mindset to a renewed mind. "And do not be conformed to this world, but be transformed by the renewing of your mind, so that you may prove what the will of God is, that which is good and acceptable and perfect" (Rom 12:2). When the Word of God becomes personal revelation through the ministry of the Holy Spirit, combined with the determination to live holy, transformation happens.

Ephesians 4:23–24 states, "and that you be renewed in the spirit of your mind, and put on the new self, which in *the likeness of* God has been created in righteousness and holiness of the truth." God desires for us to live a life of freedom and holiness (Jn 10:10). Out of His amazing and great love, God gives us free will and invites us to partner with Him in living out this life as one reflecting holiness (1 Pt 1:15–16). A holy life is a separated life, one that is separated from the "perverse generation" unto God (Phil 2:15).

God provides an open door into His family through which we may enter and form a relationship with Him. When the focus shifts from sin consciousness to Holy Spirit consciousness, we can hear and obey Him. "For God has not called us for the purpose of impurity, but in sanctification. So, he who rejects *this* is not rejecting man but the God who gives His Holy Spirit to you" (1 Thes 4:7–8). Holy Spirit brings truth to light, gives guidance and direction, and empowers believers to live holy lives.

Marriage Covenant

We commonly hear the words marriage covenant and assume that the Bible makes a point of it, especially among people who insist that divorce is never permissible because it breaks a covenant. Malachi 2:14 is the only place where marriage is referred to as a covenant. Nevertheless, if we examine the process and even ceremonies of marriage, we can easily conclude that it has all of the attributes of covenant.

Ceremonies vary among cultures, but essentially the two who marry make a public declaration before witnesses of life-long commitment to each other. Each person's vow is a unilateral covenant in that it makes a declaration of promise to love, honor, and cherish the spouse for life. Typically, there is a token like a ring given as a seal of the commitment. Some weddings in various cultures include such things as dowries, bride price, and pre-nuptial agreements.

When a couple seeks to marry, they have hope for building a happy life together. They need models for them to see what a life-long happy marriage looks like. They need to hear the testimonies of victories in the face of life's trials where people worked out their differences and were better for it. They need the tools of communication and relationship. But most of all, they need a vision of God's plan for marriage—a mutual understanding of what a covenant between them means for them.

Marriage between a man and a woman is limited to this life, not eternity as Christ and the Church. Consequently, imperfect beings find themselves having to negotiate how to live in harmony with one another. In the best of circumstances, marriage should be based on intimacy, trust, and faithfulness. When unrepentant sin enters the relationship, trust breaks down. The slippery slope leads to breaking the marriage covenant.

Sadly, not all marriages work out the way the couple envisioned it on the wedding day. Divorce in recent history has become so commonplace, that in general, it does not have the same social impact of shame and ostracism that it did long ago. Perhaps that same attitude accounts for so many young couples cohabiting without marriage. Couples usually do not enter into marriage with the intent to try out a living arrangement and call it quits if things get complicated.

The impact of divorce on individual lives and families is truly devastating. The break-up of a marriage is a disaster on so many levels—spiritually, emotionally, economically, socially, and even physically. Each case has its own complications, but the cases of shattered lives is far more than not. Individuals are heartbroken. Families are split and often form animosity towards each other. Stress and anguish can be physically debilitating and depressing. Children are shuffled back and forth between parents or never see one of the parents.

The breakdown of traditional family as an institution has been a catalyst for change in society as a whole—regardless of religious affiliations or beliefs—often negative change. As a consequence, modern family life has a new face—broken families, blended families, single-parent families, guardian-parent families, same-sex parent families, and possibly more. These new configurations may work for some, but too often, they are rife with problems. Society in general is changed and challenged with the repercussions of the disintegration of its primary social unit as it has been defined for millennia. Divorce, therefore, is still a big deal among people regardless of their religious orientation, and certainly among Bible-believing Christians where doctrines differ.

Malachi 2:13–16 give stern warnings words about ill-treatment of a spouse and frivolous divorce.

> This is another thing you do: you cover the altar of the Lord with tears, with weeping and with groaning, because He no longer regards the offering or accepts *it with* favor from your hand. Yet you say, 'For what reason?' Because the Lord has been a witness between you and the wife of your youth, against whom you have dealt treacherously, though she is your companion and your wife by covenant. But not one has done *so* who has a remnant of the Spirit. And what did *that* one *do* while he was seeking a godly offspring? Take heed then to your spirit, and let no one deal treacherously against the wife of your youth. For I hate divorce," says the Lord, the God of Israel, "and him who covers his garment with wrong," says the Lord of hosts. "So take heed to your spirit, that you do not deal treacherously (Mal 2:13–16).

It is clear from this passage that He is addressing abusive relationships that leads to divorce. God is clear about His attitude on divorce—He hates it. But He does not forbid it. This is significant, particularly from the perspective of abused spouses. Nobody likes divorce, except perhaps attorneys who specialize in high profile cases.

In the Malachi 2 text, God is addressing the practice of dissipated men divorcing their wives for unjust causes.[16] To take this portion of Scripture as an injunction to forbid divorce in all cases is simply misrepresenting the text. We can all agree that divorce is not God's best for a marriage, but breaking the marriage covenant to spare someone spousal abuse is merciful. This follows the Hebrew principle of *pikuach nefesh*—to preserve an endangered person or animal supersedes all religious injunctions and actions that are normally forbidden (*mitzvah lo ta'aseh* – command to not act) like working on the Sabbath.

In Mt 12:8–14, Jesus was accused of breaking the Sabbath to heal a man. His response was in keeping with this principle of *pikuach nefesh*. "How much more valuable then is a man than a sheep! So then, it is lawful to do good on the Sabbath" (Mt. 12:12). Preserving an endangered life always takes precedence over law.

In terms of biblical standards, some subscribe to the "death alone" ideology, whereby only death can legitimately end a marriage regardless of the circumstances. This view holds that even when one is divorced, remarriage is forbidden until the former spouse dies. This perspective does not account for issues of abandonment, abuse, and infidelity, and potentially it victimizes the victim. Some hold to the "only in cases of adultery" as the only provision for divorce based on the limited interpretation of Mt 5:32. This view also does not allow for spousal abandonment and spousal abuse.

In the event of spousal abuse, forgiveness is required of all believers, but continuing to live in an environment being subject to abusive suffering

---

16 In Orthodox Jewish practice, only men may obtain a divorce. Once he obtains the divorce decree, he then gives the woman a *get* or *gett* (document granting divorce and that adultery no longer applies to their status). A woman may petition the rabbinic court to require her husband to give her a divorce, but it is given only under unusual circumstances and rarely granted.

is neither the requirement for forgiveness, nor God's best for the health and well-being of His people. Forgiveness and faithfulness is ideal in all relationships, but when vows of honor, protection, and esteem are broken, the marriage covenant is broken long before the legal action of divorce is complete. The divorce decree is only the coffin nail in the marriage cold and dead, and legally serves to free the couple from one another.

While not condoning frivolous divorce actions or unwillingness to work at developing a good marriage, too often Church leaders condemn the victim of abuse to remain in a potentially dangerous marriage situation for the sake of religious legalism. When trust is violated and self-gratification takes priority over affection and respect, it is just as bad as, and possibly worse, than adultery. When conditions of mistrust, despair, alienation, and coercion become insurmountable and no longer tolerable, divorce is not only inevitable, but may actually be a responsible decision.

Church leadership for divorced people, particularly in light of the 1 Tim 3:2 injunction of "husband of one wife," is an issue in some Christian circles. Its varying interpretations is especially charged when applied to divorce. Is Paul speaking of divorce and remarriage, or is this about polygamy (having multiple wives)? In the ancient world, polygamy was not forbidden by law as it is in ours, but the 1 Tim 3:2 injunction implies that polygamy would complicate matters for church leadership. This would be more in keeping with Paul's preference for celibacy among ministers (1 Cor 7: 7–9). Should we then extend this interpretation to remarriage after divorce?

Remarriage after divorce being interpreted as adultery (Mk 10:11–12; Lk 16:18) is the crux of the matter in the "husband of one wife" interpretation. A few possible scenarios come to mind. Suppose a divorced male pastor remarries and his former wife dies. Is his second marriage now valid and is he free from the accusations of adultery? What has really changed in the man's marital status besides the potential judgments of legalists? Suppose a Christian woman divorced before conversion and her ex-husband remarries. Is she then free to remarry due to her conversion status, and furthermore, is her divorce valid because of her former husband's "adulterous" status as a remarried man due to the exception rule? Again, nothing has changed in the marital status of the individuals.

The underlying question in the exemption rule is whether or not God is a legalist demanding the consequence of denial in church leadership or ostracism (as interpreted by some clergy, and at times contrived) in order for an individual to be righteous—works above faith. God's Word tells us that salvation is by faith alone in Christ, not by works, resulting in imparted righteousness. This does not mean that we have license or liberty to sin because God is loving and always willing to forgive—God forbid. True forgiveness, repentance (change of direction), and restoration are always the heart of God. Restoration of a marriage gone bad is possible and desirable, but it simply will not happen unless both parties are completely committed to working out their differences and to live together in a loving healthy manner with accompanying action, not only promises.

In more legalistic circles, divorce is treated as the unpardonable sin regardless of circumstances. However, if one is a new creation in Christ upon conversion and all sin has been washed clean, why would a divorce previous to conversion be the exception? Assuming divorce is a sin, why would divorce be the exception since we have access to the throne of grace for forgiveness and repentance?

Ultimately, nobody intends to divorce when entering into a marriage. The hopes and faith for a blessed life together are celebrated and fully intended. For a variety of reasons, not all marriages survive and the devastation of its demise cannot be understated. It is rarely a frivolous decision, but one wrought with guilt, confusion, and pain. Divorce and remarriage should not be an automatic accusation of adultery. Ostracism of those who have had the misfortune of experiencing divorce is not only cruel, but may actually inflict new suffering on victims already in pain.

The Church often focuses creating policies regarding the dissolubility of marriage like whether or not Christian status before marriage impacts divorce; whether or not remarriage is adultery; and denial of leadership for those having the misfortune of divorce. These issues and related judgments are certainly worth discussing and coming to some common understanding. Nevertheless, as a community of believers, the Church should also take a restorative methodology toward individuals after the fact—a more honorable approach.

For victims of divorce, a Christ-like approach of loving care for the devastated emotions, help for victims of abuse, and restorative counsel is more in keeping with Christian ethics. The church should be concerned with becoming a network of healing for those in pain and promote ways to advance healthy family relationships as preventive measures.

Many churches practice pre-marital counseling for couples, but so often these sessions are seen as just another hoop to jump through on your way to the wedding altar. Those few weeks are marginally effective at best. A strong youth initiative with mentorship and exposure to models of success earlier has a greater potential for success. Teaching and modeling righteous living according to God's Word empowered by the Holy Spirit, and exercising personal discipline to preempt relationship problems are better strategies than having to restore wholeness that results from covenant promises made and broken.

Unequally Yoked

The question about whether or not Christians should marry unbelievers or outside of their denominational stream seems to pop up when a marriage goes bad. Often the first question asked is about the couple's status in the Kingdom of God. Church folk ask, "Are they both Christians?" If one of them happens to not be Christian, 2 Cor 6:14 invariable comes up.

> Do not be bound together [yoked in KJV] with unbelievers; for what partnership have righteousness and lawlessness, or what fellowship has light with darkness? Or what harmony has Christ with Belial, or what has a believer in common with an unbeliever? Or what agreement has the temple of God with idols? For we are the temple of the living God; just as God said, "I will dwell in them and walk among them; And I will be their God, and they

SHALL BE MY PEOPLE. "Therefore, COME OUT FROM THEIR MIDST AND BE SEPARATE," says the Lord. "AND DO NOT TOUCH WHAT IS UNCLEAN; (2 Cor 14–17, bracketed words added).

This passage has been interpreted to mean that believers should not marry outside of their faith, including other denominational streams, other religions, no religious affiliation, or philosophies (like atheism and agnosticism). In some circles, marriage outside of one's denomination is strictly forbidden. However, is 2 Cor 6 about marriage?

First of all, what is the meaning of yoked, the word used in the King James Version? The Greek word for yoke is *heterozygeō*, a compound verb, from *heteros* (to another) and to join, especially by a yoke. A yoke is a wooden crosspiece that is fastened over the necks of two animals and attached to the plow or cart that they are to pull. The various uses of the word yoke in Scripture are as follows:

- Yoked animals for plowing
- Metaphorically for bondage, slavery (Acts 15:10), 1 Tim 6:1, Lv 26:13, Gal 5:1)
- Bondservice to masters (1 Ti 6:1)
- Submission to authority (Mt 11:29, 30)
- Troublesome laws imposed (Acts 15:10)
- A balance of scales (Rev 6:5)

The word *yoke* is NEVER used in Scripture to refer to marriage. In verse 2 Cor 6:14, it is used metaphorically to address the partnership of idolatry to Christianity.

The context of 2 Cor 6: 14–18 describes the yoking that it addresses. It includes righteousness and unrighteousness joining as partners, (v. 14); harmony of Christ and Belial—name of Satan meaning "worthless" or "wicked," (v. 15); and God's temple (believers) with idols, (v. 16). Syncretism of pagan ideology and tradition, the context of this passage, was a major issue in the early church as many Gentiles came to faith.

A case can be made that in a broad sense that marriage is a type of partnership, but using the passage to determine whether either of the couple is "unrighteous" or pagan is seldom discernable, especially when both claim Christianity. Branding someone as unrighteous because they belong to a different denominational sect is not in keeping with Christian values.

Furthermore, the relationship of marriage as described by Scripture is that of the couple lovingly submitting to one another, becoming one, not merely bound or yoked. Also, if one applies verse 14 to marriage, verse 17 should also have to apply, which would tell the believer to come out and separate. The passage is telling the Corinthians to separate themselves from their former idolatrous traditions.

What if neither the married man nor woman is a believer when married, and then one of them comes to faith in Christ? If the "unequally yoked" injunction is a law, are they to separate? Clearly, that is ridiculous. First Corinthians 7:12–17 gives instructions to the Corinthians who had issues of "mixed" marriages—believers with unbelievers. The principle of peace is the key. If they can live in peace, so be it. If not and they separate, they are not in bondage.

Common sense would say that marriage between people of unlike faith has potential for difficulty, and is not wise, but it is not forbidden in the New Testament as it is among Israelites in the Old Testament. Understandably, people with like-minded faith have a better shot at working out the tensions of marriage than ones who have oppositional views. That is also true of the couple's philosophy of finance, child-rearing practices, and the relationships with extended families. The more the couple can see "eye to eye," on life's issues, the better chance for harmonious living.

The principle of two people who are not in harmony with their beliefs from the outset are bound to have struggles ahead. Too often promises are made during the engagement, especially regarding child-rearing in a particular faith, and then later broken. Wisdom and good counsel would say to reconsider such a union, but 2 Cor 6:14 is not a proof text for it.

Marriage, as a Covenant Metaphor

Marriage is a metaphor to describe the relationship of intimacy and faithfulness of Christ toward His Church, an eternal covenant relationship. Jesus refers to Himself as the bridegroom in Jn 3:29 and in the Parable of the Ten Virgins in Mt 25:1–13. The point being that the Church must keep itself focused and prepared for the coming of Christ—keeping our spiritual eyes fixed on Jesus, the author and finisher of our faith (Heb 12:2). Jesus is ever faithful in His commitment to the Bride.

As individual members of the Body of Christ, we must be keep our spiritual eyes in covenant with Jesus. If the spiritual eyes begin to wander to something else, it is the slippery slope to the break of that covenant, the result like spiritual adultery. It is as idolatry. This is why the first of the two commandments Jesus gave is to love God with all of your heart, mind, soul, and strength (Mk 12:30).

An example of the spiritual adultery among God's people is the story in Exodus where Moses goes to the mountain at Mount Sinai where God gives the commandments and ordinances for His People (Ex 20). Moses spent some time on the mountain and the people became impatient and were unsure of what had become of Moses. Their faith was derailed. They demanded that Aaron cast an idol that they would worship and set before them in their journey, which Aaron did.

They turned their eyes from the Lord and put it on the idol that was familiar to them in Egypt. The gold calf was an image they knew well—the cow goddess Hathor, a major goddess throughout Egypt that personified motherhood, love, and nurture. They chose Hathor above God. Even Aaron, the brother of Moses, allowed the people to get out of control (Ex 32:25). About 3,000 of them lost their lives that day and Moses interceded on behalf of the remaining people. Ultimately, all of the people over twenty years of age who left Egypt died in the wilderness and did not enter the Promised Land, except for Joshua and Caleb. Moses took the people out of Egypt but could not take Egypt out of the people. They were responsible for their beliefs.

In Eph 5:22–33, Paul compares the Church to the bride and Jesus as the bridegroom. As the Bride of Christ, the Church is committed to fidelity just as in a marriage the couple pledge themselves to fidelity toward one another. Colossians 3:5 tells us, "Therefore consider the members of your earthly body as dead to immorality, impurity, passion, evil desire, and greed, which amounts to idolatry." These kinds of acts happen when spiritual and even natural eyes wander to places where God does not dwell. Eyes no longer behold the King of Glory, but yearn for something else. Destruction always follows because the idol cannot provide what God does. "Therefore, my beloved, flee from idolatry" (2 Cor 10:14). Obedience to a covenant of the Lord positions you to receive His word, His direction and guidance, His provision, and His legacy (Lv 26:3–12).

The Good News

The good news is that it's not too late to live a holy life, separated unto God. He gives forgiveness and grace for repentance. If you have an addiction to pornography, you can be set free by the power of the Holy Spirit. Ask God for forgiveness and strength. Then make the determination to stay free. It will require you to repent—which means walking away from persons, places, or things that present temptation. "Now flee from youthful lusts and pursue righteousness, faith, love *and* peace, with those who call on the Lord from a pure heart" (2 Tim 2:22). It's not sin to be tempted; it is to entertain it and then yield.

If you have suffered the break of a marriage covenant, your life is not over. If you need to forgive and/or receive forgiveness, don't delay. It opens the path to the beginning of a new way to live. Restoration of your marriage may happen, but if it does not, your personal restoration need not be in jeopardy. God's love and provision are there to help and sustain you.

Prayer

Heavenly Father, thank you that You care for me. Your desire is for me to walk in freedom and holiness. I ask forgiveness for the sin in my life (whatever it is, name it – bitterness, gossip, pornography, abusing a spouse, etc.) that I have caused someone else. I receive Your grace and strength to stay free from the hold it had on me. I submit to You, Holy Spirit, who leads and guides me to all truth and godly living. I ask forgiveness for any harm I may have caused. Lord, Your ways are higher than mine and I seek to follow after You. I depend on your Spirit to direct my life so that it would be pleasing to you. I thank you, Lord, that You hear my prayer, in Jesus' Name.

GUIDE: QUESTIONS FOR DISCUSSION OR JOURNALING

Chapter Five: Intimate Covenants

1. Do you think Job's strategy for purity is relevant today?
2. Considering the enormous influence of the entertainment industry and the pressure within a society that has compromised the moral imperatives of the past, what are some ways the Church can foster purity for its youth?
3. Is marriage an adequate metaphor for the relationship between Christ and the Church?
4. What are some ingredients to keep a healthy covenant relationship in marriage?

NOTES

NOTES

Marketplace Covenants

―∞―

IT'S NOT JUST BUSINESS; IT'S PERSONAL

WHEN THE PACKAGE FINALLY ARRIVED in the mail, she opened it with anticipation that it would be the perfect gift. She pulled out the packing materials and found a pile of broken china cups and saucers. It seems to have been packed right, but the shipping process may have been unusually rough. She had paid for the shipping with insurance in case of damage, but the postage on the package showed it was not done. The sender had not insured the package, so she could not put in a claim with the shipper. How should the scenario end? Choose an ending.

   a. She calls the company to complain, leaves multiple recording and never gets a call back. Completely frustrated, she gives up and goes shopping.
   b. She calls the company and gets a customer service agent who is somewhere in another country. She can't understand the accent and has such difficulty communicating, she hangs up. She cries and goes shopping.
   c. She throws the box of broken china in the garbage and goes shopping.
   d. She calls her credit card company and hopes they can help her get a refund. In the meantime, she goes shopping.
   e. She calls the company, gets a customer service representative on the phone, and they send her a new box of china.

Retail therapy is not the answer to bad business. Honest business dealings would require the seller to refund the customer in full including shipping charges or arrange to resend an equal replacement.

The frustration of feeling cheated and victimized in dishonest business dealings can be infuriating, especially when there is no recourse for restitution. Seeking recompense, even through legal means with uncooperative parties compounds the aggravation, but it is also bad business practice. Reputable companies will usually guarantee their products because they want to keep their customer base. Repeat business is at the core of successful retail business.

The underlying motivations of dishonest business are greed and fear—greed for profits and fear of loss of profits. The prophet Amos characterizes dishonest business as predatory. He declares,

> Hear this, you who trample the needy, to do away with the humble
> of the land, saying, "When will the new moon be over,
> So that we may sell grain,
> And the sabbath, that we may open the wheat *market*,
> To make the bushel smaller and the shekel bigger,
> And to cheat with dishonest scales,
> So as to buy the helpless for money
> And the needy for a pair of sandals,
> And *that* we may sell the refuse of the wheat (Am 8:4–6)?

Amos prophesies ultimate doom to those who engage in unrighteous activity. In the last line of Amos 8, he declares, "They will fall and not rise again."

Truth and integrity in business dealing is not only right to the fair-minded, it is also godly (Lv 19:35–36). Proverbs 20:10 states, "Differing weights and differing measures, Both of them are abominable to the LORD," and Prv 11:1, "A false balance is an abomination to the LORD, But a just weight is His delight." In current times, fair practices for business would include such issues as consumer protection, copyright protection, disclosure of ingredients, compliance with trade laws both national and international, rejection of slipshod work or substandard materials, and compliance with all tax laws.

Caveat emptor (Latin for "Let the buyer beware.") is a phrase that means the buyer makes a purchase at his/her own risk (product "as is") and is responsible for checking any imperfections or defects. On the surface, it appears to exonerate the seller of all responsibility for condition of the item. Although this is a guiding principle for any purchaser, it does not entirely shield the seller from accountability from making false representations of a product and that it has implied warranties to do what the product is designed to do. For example, the implied warranty of purchasing a jar of peanut butter is that it has peanuts and is edible. As a result of consumer protection laws, *caveat vendor* (Latin for "Let the seller beware.") is more often the case in modern marketplace practice. The greater responsibility of product authenticity and truth in lending falls on the seller.

The consumer is not morally free from honest dealings either. Upright exchange means such things as returning funds when the teller gives you more change than should be for the purchase; having legitimate reasons for complaint; and complying with return-of-item policies. Although a good business reputation is important, God's view of integrity is greater. God takes delight in His people dealing honestly with one another and the world (Prv 11:1).

BUSINESS PARTNERING

They knew each other for three years, and enjoyed times of socializing regularly. Both claim to be believing Christians, regularly attending and being involved in their respective churches. They each saw a business opportunity, but neither one had the resource to engage alone. They decided to form a partnership, each bringing what the other needed. With great anticipation for success, they dove into their projects with gusto. After all, they are Christians. What could go wrong?

Two years into the business, one of them realizes that the other was embezzling and diverting funds, thereby swindling the other. Heartbroken, angry, and no funds to show for the work effort, the cheated partner dissolves their enterprise. He or she walks away disgraced, disillusioned, and determined to never trust again. It's a scenario too often repeated.

The greatest lesson learned from bad partnerships is "And we beseech you, brethren, to know them which labour among you, and are over you in the Lord, and admonish you; And to esteem them very highly in love for their work's sake. And be at peace among yourselves" (1 Thes 5:12-13, KJV). Knowing the one who labors among you means that you fully know their work ethic, integrity, and skills—even Christians. We cannot assume integrity by claims of religious beliefs. At best, it is always wise to form business partnership contracts with specificity and practice regular accountability as the business progresses.

Abraham and Abimelech, Philistine king of Gerar, provide a biblical example of business dealings. They had some history. Sarah was beautiful and desirable. In order to prevent the king from harming Abraham to take Sarah, Abraham and Sarah conspired to tell Abimelech that she is his sister as they did previously with the pharaoh in Egypt. Abimelech plans to take Sarah as a wife, but he has a dream and the truth is revealed. Abimelech sends Abraham away with goods and wealth. Before they leave, Abraham prays for Abimelech and his household (they were barren as consequence of Abimelech's designs on Sarah), and they were healed—the first recorded healing in Scripture.

Later, Abraham and Abimelech enter into another round of dealings (Gn 21: 22–34). Abimelech asks Abraham to swear he would not deal falsely with him or his descendants. Abraham agrees, but then he complains that his wells were seized by Abimelech's servants. Abimelech claims no knowledge of the situation. Abraham and Abimelech resolve their difference by making a bilateral covenant. Abraham would deal honestly with Abimelech and Abimelech would not interfere with the wells. The covenant was bilateral and for perpetuity—ongoing with their descendants. Abraham gave Abimelech seven ewes and to seal the deal. Abraham then planted a tamarisk tree[17] there as a memorial of that covenant and called the place Beersheba (meaning "well of oath").

The critical term of the covenant they made is that of perpetuity. The covenant they struck was not only active in their lifetimes, but they committed their descendants to honor the covenant as well. Their covenant was challenged after Abraham died. Isaac found that the Philistines, who did not honor the covenant, stopped up the wells his father had dug (Gn 26:18–33). Isaac redug two wells, but it created conflict with the Philistines. After digging the third well, Abimelech[18] comes to Isaac to resolve the problem. They make a peace covenant, sealed with a feast. The sons thereby honored the promises made by their fathers.

The story of the covenant between Abraham and Abimelech and later involving Isaac, is significant as a model of business integrity. Whatever is agreed upon and covenanted, should be upheld to the letter. If compromised, it should be restored, corrected, or resolved based on the terms of the original promises.

God's covenants are upheld to the letter—every jot and tittle.[19] His integrity is pure and upright. We can rely on God's covenants with utmost authority and credibility. Without the assurance and history of the trustworthiness of God's covenants, we would have no grounds for faith. "But you shall remember the Lord your God for it is He who is giving you power to make wealth, that He may confirm His covenant which He swore to your fathers, as it is this day" (Dt 8:18). God's principles are for all peoples for all times. Family, neighbors, friends, and even strangers should

---

17 Tamarisk trees grow on saline soils with deep taproots and is good for reclaiming desertification. It's a good choice for a memorial marker because its deep roots speak of permanence long after the event has happened.

18 Abimelech means "son of the king" and is probably a royal title similar to pharaoh in Egypt. The Abimelech that Isaac encounters is most likely the son of the one Abraham encountered.

19 "For verily I say unto you, Till heaven and earth pass, one jot or one tittle shall in no wise pass from the law, till all be fulfilled (Mt 5:18, KJV)." A jot is the least letter of the alphabet or the smallest piece of writing, a precursor to the dot of an *i*. Tittle is a small stroke on a letter indicating an accent or dotted *i*. The point of the quote is that the tiniest part of God's Word shall be fulfilled.

be able to rely on our credibility as well. God is delighted with honor and integrity in business transactions among His people (Prv 11:1).

EVERYONE'S BUSINESS

When one of my nephews was just a teenager, he found a bag in the parking lot of a fast food restaurant where he worked part-time after school. He looked inside the bag and was surprised to find thousands of dollars in cash and some checks. Because of the checks, he was able to find out who the owner of the money was and he returned the entire amount to the person without any calculating motives or expectations. The event even made the local newspaper.

He could easily have discarded the checks and kept the cash. In fact, some might even think he was foolish for returning the treasure. Even at that age, my nephew knew what was the right thing to do. In the long run, keeping those thousands while knowing to whom it belongs would have hurt him. Returning it positioned him for blessing, and indeed, as an adult he is blessed.

Not everyone owns a business, but everyone engages in business. In some way, we are all involved in commerce—shopping, working, banking, trading. Integrity in the marketplace is not only for business owners. It is for everyone—employers, employees, purveyors, shoppers, and even volunteers.

Words like honesty, integrity, credibility, and reliability are not only vague ideas or suggestions in the workplace or marketplace. They are meaningful in affirming your testimony of God's presence in your life. They affirm the possibilities of God in their lives.

The list of worker and shopper abuses can be very long as most people can attest. Here is a short list of the lack of honesty and integrity that occurs in everyday business:

- Not returning funds that were given as incorrect change at a store register.

- Using the company's copy machine for personal use
- Pilfering office supplies (paper clips, rubber bands, staples, paper)
- Returning clothing to stores after having worn them to an event
- Regularly arriving at the workplace late or leaving early, even a few minutes
- Taking unjustifiable extra time for lunch or breaks
- Manipulating resources unfairly to get ahead

These may not be grand scale larceny, but they certainly are not godly and they erode a person's testimony. They become a slippery slope to justifying unrighteousness.

God has something to say about the workplace. In writing to the Ephesians, Paul addresses the relationship between workers and their employers. Paul refers to masters and slaves in work relationship because of the context of the society in which he lived. Slaves were a commonplace reality in most of the known world at that time. Obviously, we do NOT encourage or believe people should be enslaved under any circumstances.

> Slaves [workers],[20] be obedient to those who are your masters [employers] according to the flesh, with fear and trembling, in the sincerity of your heart, as to Christ; not by way of eyeservice, as men-pleasers, but as slaves [servants] of Christ, doing the will of God from the heart. With good will render service, as to the Lord, and not to men knowing that whatever good thing each one does, this he will receive back from the Lord, whether slave or free [regardless of status]. And masters [employers], do the same things to them, and give up threatening, knowing that both their Master

---

20 The word slave in Eph 6:5 is not intended to approved of or validate slavery in any form. The context of the passage is about work ethics from both the employer and the employee perspective, which is applicable in this century to employer-employee relationships. It is a heartrending situation that slavery and human trafficking is still a reality in the twenty-first century throughout the world. Several ministries and secular organizations are working hard to combat and alleviate such suffering.

[Jesus] and yours is in heaven, and there is no partiality with Him (Eph 6:5–9, bracketed words added).

The issues of slavery and human trafficking have come to the forefront in recent years, but it still happens too often. That being said, the principles that are laid out in this passage are about fairness and integrity in employer-employee relationships, accountability, and responsibility.

This also includes the administrative departments in the church as a work place. Few things are more upsetting than when church personnel (leaders, employees) do not act honorably in their administrative dealings. When church leaders are found to be dishonest, it profoundly affects the community of believers, causing deep hurt. The expectation is that of all places, the Church should be a model of ethics and morality. When that is compromised, it is a deep betrayal.

Besides the unwritten code of workplace ethics—be polite, be on time, cooperate, do your job, don't abuse privileges—many professions and employment situations involve contracts where the duties and responsibilities of each party is spelled out. In some cases, unions and professional associations are representatives of the work force as a body and enter into contractual agreements with employers on behalf of the union members. But even when a paper contract does not exist, God's expectation is about integrity. Employees are responsible for fulfilling the tasks for which they are hired to the best of their ability as unto the Lord. Employers are to treat their employees with respect. In living this ethic, the Lord promises favor—the "good thing each one does" will be received back from the Lord.

The Good News

Psalm 15:4 states, ". . . But who honors those who fear the Lord He swears to his own hurt and does not change." To swear to your own hurt means that it may cost an inconvenience or even some serious resources to fulfill a promise. Nevertheless, a word given is a bond of action to that word. It is so with God and should be so among His people, both in personal and business matters. The good news is that ethical dealing is sowing good seed that will produce a good harvest. It's a new day and it's not too late to do what is right.

Prayer

Thank you, Lord, that You care about all that concerns my life. It is Your desire that I prosper in all that I set my hands to do and that I walk uprightly in all my dealings. I repent of any and all actions in the workplace that have not been honorable and I receive your forgiveness. I also forgive anyone who has not acted honorable toward me, anyone who has cheated me, or has been dishonest. I ask you, Lord, to reveal Your ways to them, and You increase my awareness to deal honorably in all things. I believe and receive your Word that you lead and guide me in the workplace and it brings you glory in Jesus' Name.

GUIDE: QUESTIONS FOR DISCUSSION OR JOURNALING

Chapter Six: Marketplace Covenants

1. In what ways do business practices impact success or failure?
2. In what ways should employer-employee relationships reflect principles of the Kingdom of God?
3. How should a Christian handle abuses witnessed in business? Are there legitimate options?
4. National attention has been given to certain businesses that have been the target of law suits because the business owners' beliefs conflicted with the demands of particular consumers on the business (Examples: a bakery refusing to bake a wedding cake for a gay couple; paying for employee's health insurance that covers abortion). What are your thoughts about these cases?

NOTES

NOTES

Remembering Covenants

THE MEMORY OF BROTHER CLYDE Jones always makes me smile. It was 1976, at the tail end of the Jesus Movement, and I had recently dedicated my life to be a follower of Jesus. Brother Jones was a member of the small congregation in New Jersey. Everybody in church called him Brother Jones, so we did too. Everybody loved Brother Jones.

Brother Jones loved to worship. He was nearly 90 years old at the time, and always came to church with his violin. When the music began, he would take out his violin and join in with the pianist from his seat. Every now and then, when the music was particularly lively, he would break out into a little dance. He led a simple lifestyle of faith, believing God for all provision. Church members often brought him food because if you gave him money, he would give it away instead of buying groceries and then not have food.

On occasion, Brother Jones joined us at our home for a meal after church services ended. He would regale us with stories of his ministry in the early half of the 1900s, particularly during the depression era. He was a traveling minister among the poor villages of Appalachia in West Virginia and Kentucky. He often told of communities tucked away in the mountains where they had no church, far away from the sophistication of cities and towns. He would go into the local saloon and preach the gospel. The people would receive Christ and convert the saloon it into a church.

Remembering this precious brother and the many testimonies of God's provision and grace still blesses us. His stories built faith. This is the power of testimony. It reminds us of God's grace, gifts, provision, and faithfulness.

Remembering has the quality of not only bringing back the testimony of the event to the surface, but we revisit the emotional bond to that person or circumstance. It builds up and encourages faith to remember the goodness and faithfulness of God in circumstances, especially hard ones. Psalm 135:14 says, "Your name, O Lord, is everlasting, Your remembrance, O Lord, throughout all generations."

When the Israelites crossed the Jordan River to take the Promised Land under the leadership of Joshua, God spoke to Joshua and instructed him to have one man from each tribe take a stone from the middle of the Jordan. They set them in the middle of the river where the Ark of the Covenant was carried. The Israelites passed through the Jordan on dry ground. They took the twelve stones and set them up in Gilgal so that whenever the people would pass and see the stones, they would be reminded of their miraculous crossing into the Promised Land in the same manner as the Israelites crossed the sea escaping from Egypt.

The feast of Passover is a remembrance of the events of the deliverance of the Israelites from their slavery in Egypt. Every year the story is retold in Jewish homes thousands of years later. Celebrating Passover binds Jews all over the world as one people. It is the testimony of the great works of a covenant God on behalf of His people. It is also the prophetic picture of the coming of Messiah, the perfect lamb slain for the redemption of all people.

When Jesus shared the Last Supper with His disciples, He gave them an imperative of remembrance that would be carried as the central ordinance/sacrament of Christianity to this day.

> "and when He had given thanks, He broke it and said, "This is My body, which is for you; do this in remembrance of Me. In the same way *He took* the cup also after supper, saying, "This cup is the new covenant in My blood; do this, as often as you drink *it*, in remembrance of Me (1 Cor 11:24–25)."

As Christians, we drink the fruit of the vine and eat the bread again and again in remembrance of the life, sacrifice, and redemption Jesus gave on our behalf with His body and blood. We also remember how He loved and cared for His disciples as a community of believers, and the remembrance serves as the model for us to follow. As we partake in the Communion (Lord's Supper), we commune with Jesus as well as with one another. We are reminded of the two commandments of the New Covenant—to love God, and love one another.

Not all memories are delightful, but we can learn from them too. Failures can provide valuable lessons in redemption and also guidance to avoid repeating the failure. Psalm 78 brings up the failure of Ephraim.[21] After Solomon's death, the Kingdom of Israel was divided into two kingdoms. The northern was called Ephraim and southern Judah. Ephraim was continuously ruled by wicked kings and they did not keep the covenant of God.

Throughout the history of the Israelite nation, we see the cycle of sin, repentance, and restoration. God gives prosperity; people lose their fervor for God and fall into idolatry; they suffer the consequences of sin; they cry out in repentance and turn back to covenant relationship with God; God delivers them; they begin to prosper; then the cycle starts again. The remembrance of God's Covenant and His faithfulness prompted the repentance.

The Israelites of the Book are not particularly unique. Humanity's history is rife with the proclivity towards satisfying the lust of the flesh, lust of the eyes, and pride of life (1 Jn 2:16) in spite of God encounters. Prisons are crowded with repeat offenders caught in the cycle of recidivism. The power of darkness keeps unbelieving people in the bondage of sin. Remaining steadfast in a faith-filled covenant relationship with God—perseverance in the faith—keeps one from the cycle of sin.

---

21 Ephraim was the older of Joseph's two sons. Ephraim was also the name of that son's tribe as they entered into the Promised Land with Moses. Much later, upon Solomon's death, his sons divided the kingdom of Israel into the Northern and Southern Kingdoms, each including the tribes within their respective regions. The Northern Kingdom was called Ephraim and the Southern Kingdom was called Judea.

Life is but a vapor, as Jas 4:14 states. The years rush past and before you know it, you are checking the senior citizens box on government forms. Our thoughts then turn from building future success to leaving a legacy. We want to leave good things to our children and grandchildren. We want to be remembered as one who lived right and we want our posterity to know the goodness and lovingkindness of God. This is the promise to those who keep God's covenant.

Covenant-keeping is a high priority with God. Psalms, the book of worshipful songs with truth revealed in its lyrics, has much to say about covenant. It even declares precious promises for covenant-keepers. "All the paths of the Lord are lovingkindness and truth to those who keep His covenant and His testimonies" (Ps 25:10). It tells us that for those who choose to follow Him, the secret of the Lord is revealed and He makes His covenant known to them (Ps. 25:14). He calls covenant followers godly (Ps 50:5). God even says that the wicked have no right to speak of His covenant (Ps. 50:16). God does not violate His covenant, nor does He alter His word (Ps 89:34). God provides a tremendous promise in Psalm 103 to covenant keepers, for themselves and for their descendants. "But the lovingkindness of the Lord is from everlasting to everlasting on those who fear Him, And His righteousness to children's children, to those who keep His covenant And remember His precepts to do them" (Ps 103:17–18).

As a New Covenant believer, keeping covenant means communing with God, hearing Him and following His lead. "He has sent redemption to His people; He has ordained His covenant forever; holy and awesome is His name. The fear of the Lord is the beginning of wisdom; a good understanding have all those who do *His commandments*; His praise endures forever" (Ps 111:9–10).

As covenant followers, we have covenant blessing of all that God offers His people. That includes healing, protection, prosperity, assurance of eternal life (salvation), heirship/family membership with Him, direct access to God, intimacy, authority, purity, and empowerment for service. As we bring forward remembrance of God's covenant, our focus shifts from self to selfless, from sin consciousness to God consciousness, from bondage to freedom, from mourning to joy, from death to eternal life.

The Good News

When we pray, we bring God's Word before Him, not because God forgets. The omniscient God surely does not forget His Word and promises. When we do so, we remind ourselves of the times and seasons God has delivered us out of darkness and destruction because of His great love and faithfulness. As the testimony of God's power and love are retold, it encourages our faith. What could be more powerful that praying God's own Words regarding your circumstance. Renew your mind—align your thinking with the Word of God. What are you believing God for? Find His Word on the matter in Scripture and bring it to God in remembrance. Thank God for His Word and for His loving provision for His sons and daughters.

Prayer

Lord, your Word declares _____ (fill in) about _____ (fill in). Your Word is sure and I believe what You have said. Thank you, Lord, that Your Word brings life and godliness to me. By faith, I receive what You have said and I stand on it in Jesus' Name.

GUIDE: QUESTIONS FOR
DISCUSSION OR JOURNALING

—⋙—

Chapter Seven: Remembering the Covenant

1. Think about traditions you observe. What role do these traditions have in your family and friend relationships?
2. Jesus gave the injunction, "Do this in remembrance of Me," at the Last Supper. What was he asking His followers to remember and why is it important? What does communion mean for you?
3. Why is remembering and telling the testimony of God's works of the past important?
4. Which covenants of God have been significant for you?

NOTES

NOTES

Putting the "I" Into Integrity

—ɯ—

REDEMPTION AND RESTORATION ARE ALWAYS God's goals for humanity. Whether through narratives, poetry, or teachings, the ultimate conclusion of Scripture is that God desires people to come to Him, be made whole, and have fellowship with Him. God's stated desire is for us to live a life of holiness—separated unto God (1 Pt 1:16) and to be transformed into the image of Christ. "But we all, with unveiled face, beholding as in a mirror the glory of the Lord, are being transformed into the same image from glory to glory, just as from the Lord, the Spirit" (2 Cor 3:18).

God sees all and knows all—both the obvious and what is hidden (Eccl 12:13–14). As free-will agents, we choose to receive God's grace for forgiveness, repentance and restoration. "If we confess our sins, He is faithful and righteous to forgive us our sins and to cleanse us from all unrighteousness" (1 Jn 1:9). Each person has the opportunity to confront the need for forgiveness and repentance from evil works—including breaking well-intentioned covenants. This is not a word of condemnation. It is a snap to reality and freedom. The light of the Holy Spirit shines on habits that keep us bound—things that prevent us from God's best. The ever-faithful, covenant-keeping God gives us grace to change. That's good news!

Although it keeps society relatively stable, living ethically and keeping promises may have little to do with God if it is only intellectual assent. Unless one is a sociopath in need of deliverance, people already know what socially acceptable and unacceptable behavior looks like—the knowledge of what society deems criminal. The difficulty with living in society's concept of ethics, however, is that the boundaries are continually shifting and becoming muddy. The prohibition era of the "Roaring Twenties" and its aftermath (1920–1933) and the social revolution of the 1960s are great examples of shifting mores, scruples, and traditions. What may have once been good is now bad, and behaviors once considered shameful are at the very least, acceptable or tolerated. God's Word, on the other hand, is stable and completely trustworthy forever.

We tend to hold church leaders to a higher moral and ethical standard than others in covenant promise-keeping. We expect them to be of "good reputation, full of the Spirit and wisdom" (Acts 4:3), along with other character traits listed in 1 Tim 3:2–4 and Ti 1:7. The belief is that they have both the knowledge and calling to teach and model God's ways for the people they serve to help them grow—rightfully so. Leaders are expected to be able to hear from God and have the commitment to follow His voice. These qualities—hearing God and obeying His voice—however, are not limited to the availability and responsibility of leaders. They are for all believers. Covenant-keeping is for everyone.

The path to holy living and covenant-keeping is more than simply following rules or subscribing to an intellectual ethic. What makes the difference is that it is not motivated by avoidance of bad behavior or even rewards of goodness, but rather by the desire to please God. It is motivated by receiving God's love and loving Him in return. It requires us to hear and heed the voice of God through the many ways He speaks to us—through His written Word, prayer, prophecy, dreams and visions, His audible voice, the inner witness, and more. God is not silent. Hebrews 10:15–17 declares the core promise of the New Covenant in that God speaks to His people and guides them in righteousness.

> And the Holy Spirit also testifies to us; for after saying, 'This is the covenant that I will make with them after those days, says the Lord: I will put my laws upon their heart, and on their mind I will

write them,' he then says, 'and their sins and their lawless deeds I will remember no more' (Heb 10:15–17).

The desire to be a covenant-keeper begins with as you being willing to hear from the Holy Spirit regarding an issue that has come to your attention—a personal inventory. Is God speaking to you regarding any of the following?

- Being mindful of your commitments and keeping your promises.
- Being proactive on issues of personal purity.
- Cherishing and stewarding relational covenants like friendship and marriage.
- Dealing honorably in the marketplace.
- Keeping God in remembrance.

This is a call to personal action—to purposefully put the "I" (self) into integrity. Ask yourself, "Where do I locate myself in these issues, and to what am I willing to commit when I hear from the Spirit?" Answering honestly to yourself begins the journey of living in a Christ-like manner, journey well worth taking.

The Good News

Wherever we are in our journey with God, there is more available to us—more revelation of God through communion with Him because of the New Covenant; more revelation of our character strengths, weaknesses, and even sin through the voice of the Holy Spirit; and the promise of empowerment by the Holy Spirit to grow in grace and truth. Covenant blessings await the hearer and doer. That includes everything we need for holy living – healing, protection, provision, assurance of eternal life (salvation), heirship/family relationship in the Kingdom of God, intimacy with direct access to God, authority, purity, and empowerment to keep our promises to God and "pinky promises" with one another. What a huge benefit package!

Prayer

Lord, your grace is sufficient for me in all matters of my life. I believe you and your Word regarding discernment, strength, and courage to change whatever I need to correct in my life. Because your name is a strong tower, I run into it and find safety (Prv 18:10). I am a sheep in Your pasture (Jn 10:3) and know your voice. I submit my thoughts, my will, and my words to Your will, words, and ways so that I grow in grace and truth, and that I fulfill all that You have called me to do. I rely on Your help and guidance to live as a person of integrity. You are the Lord of my life. Thank you, Lord, for your great love.

GUIDE: QUESTIONS FOR DISCUSSION OR JOURNALING

Chapter Eight: Putting the "I" into Integrity

1. In what ways is personal integrity necessary in public or secular dealings?
2. Take a personal inventory and determine areas both major and minor where integrity has been somewhat lacking. What one thing are you willing to work on?
3. What are some things you can do to hold yourself accountable to your word?
4. How has a deeper understanding of covenant helped you understand the faithfulness of God?

NOTES

NOTES

NOTES

NOTES

ABOUT THE AUTHOR

EVA HAS BEEN AN ORDAINED minister for decades and has been involved in multiple facets of ministry including church planting, developing biblical studies curricula, and equipping believers through teaching, and preaching. Her style of ministry is engaging and energetic. In her presentation, even the most difficult biblical text become alive and easy to understand. Ministry assignments, imperatives, and calling have taken her to such places as Germany, China, Israel, Mozambique, Brazil, and Philippines, as well as throughout the U.S.

Concurrent with ministry, Eva also enjoyed a successful forty-year career as an educator, staff developer, education consultant, and author of professional education publications. She earned her B.A. and M.A. from William Paterson University in education and communication arts, and leadership certification from Fairleigh Dickenson University. Having now retired from secular education, Eva now focuses all of her energy on Kingdom initiatives that includes writing and ministering as God opens doors of opportunity.

Eva earned a doctorate degree in ministry from United Theological Seminary where her research specialized in the doctrine of impartation. Her book, *The Power of Touch: Divine Impartation Through Touch*, an in-depth study of the doctrine of impartation of the Holy Spirit has been well received in both the academic community and general public. Her blog, *Things Revealed* on her website, evabenevento.com, offers articles on a variety of topics as well.

Eva's deepest desire is for individuals grow and fulfill their destinies in the power of the Holy Spirit. Her core values are simply stated as "HIS in the Kingdom: Holiness, Integrity, and Servanthood" to glorify the Father, Jesus, and the Holy Spirit.

Dr. Eva Benevento is available for speaking engagements.
Please contact her at dresb15@gmail.com or
Dr. Eva Benevento,
P.O. Box 613, Ramsey, NJ 07446

From spiritual leaders to unassuming sheepherders, the laying on of hands has been a practice used by God to heal the blind and to impart spiritual gifts by everyday people when they touch each other in prayer. *The Power of Touch* explores a wealth of ancient texts to provide tangible evidence of the power that exists within the laying on of hands—a power that is available to all.

What others have said:

Every sentence in Dr. Eva Benevento's book contains a diamond of revelation. At no time will you encounter boredom as you read and absorb this historical documentation of Scriptural truth.
Dr. Bobbie Jean Merck, A Great Love, Toccoa, Georgia

Eva Benevento tackles this subject with intellectual and biblical integrity, and captures the spiritual power of this practice. She has great respect for the spiritual power imparted that emanates from the Holy Spirit in the laying on of hands as well as the danger it presents in New Age practices. This is a must read for anyone serious about moving in the power of the Holy Spirit through the laying on of hands.
Barbara Yoder, Shekinah Regional Apostolic Center, Ann Arbor, Michigan.

Eva is a gifted writer and diligent researcher whose work provides a thorough understanding of the subject. I believe that anyone who reads *The Power of Touch* with an open mind will come to a greater realization as to how vital touch is within the ministry of the Body of Christ.
Dr. Geoff Wattoff, Centereach, New York

Available in print or Kindle. Purchase through amazon.com
or directly at:
Dr. Eva Benevento
P.O. Box 613
Ramsey, NJ 07446

NOTES

NOTES

NOTES

NOTES

NOTES